Kaplan Publishing are constantly finding new ways to make a difference to your studies and our exciting online resources really do offer something different to students looking for exam success.

This book comes with free MyKaplan online resources so that you can study anytime, anywhere

Having purchased this book, you have access to the following online study materials:

CONTENT	ACCA (including FFA, FAB, FMA)		AAT		FIA (excluding FFA, FAB, FMA)	
	Text	Kit	Text	Kit	Text	Kit
iPaper version of the book	✓	✓	✓	✓	✓	✓
Interactive electronic version of the book	✓					
Progress tests with instant answers	✓		✓			
Mock assessments online			✓	✓		
Material updates	✓	✓	✓	✓	✓	✓
Latest official ACCA exam questions		✓				
Extra question assistance using the signpost icon*		✓				
Timed questions with an online tutor debrief using the clock icon*		✓				
Interim assessment including questions and answers	✓				✓	
Technical articles	✓	✓			✓	✓

* Excludes F1, F2, F3, FFA, FAB, FMA

How to access your online resources

Kaplan Financial students will already have a MyKaplan account and these extra resources will be available to you online. You do not need to register again, as this process was completed when you enrolled. If you are having problems accessing online materials, please ask your course administrator.

If you are already a registered MyKaplan user go to www.MyKaplan.co.uk and log in. Select the 'add a book' feature and enter the ISBN number of this book and the unique pass key at the bottom of this card. Then click 'finished' or 'add another book'. You may add as many books as you have purchased from this screen.

If you purchased through Kaplan Flexible Learning or via the Kaplan Publishing website you will automatically receive an e-mail invitation to MyKaplan. Please register your details using this email to gain access to your content. If you do not receive the e-mail or book content, please contact Kaplan Flexible Learning.

If you are a new MyKaplan user register at www.MyKaplan.co.uk and click on the link contained in the email we sent you to activate your account. Then select the 'add a book' feature, enter the ISBN number of this book and the unique pass key at the bottom of this card. Then click 'finished' or 'add another book'.

Your Code and Information

This code can only be used once for the registration of one book online. This registration and your online content will expire when the final sittings for the examinations covered by this book have taken place. Please allow one hour from the time you submit your book details for us to process your request.

D0317897

Please scratch the film to access your MyKaplan code.

Please be aware that this code is case-sensitive and you will need to include the dashes within the passcode, but not when entering the ISBN. For further technical support, please visit www.MyKaplan.co.uk

KAPLAN

PUBLISHING

PREPARE FINAL ACCOUNTS FOR SOLE TRADERS AND PARTNERSHIPS

Qualifications and Credit Framework

AQ2013 Level 3 Diploma in Accounting

British Library Cataloguing-in-Publication Data

A catalogue record for this book is available from the British Library.

Published by
Kaplan Publishing UK
Unit 2, The Business Centre
Molly Millars Lane
Wokingham
Berkshire
RG41 2QZ

ISBN 978 0 85732 874 8

We are grateful to the Association of Accounting Technicians for permission to reproduce past assessment materials and example tasks based on the new syllabus. The solutions to past answers and similar activities in the style of the new syllabus have been prepared by Kaplan Publishing.

CONTENTS

INTRODUCTION

HOW TO USE THESE MATERIALS

These Kaplan Publishing learning materials have been carefully designed to make your learning experience as easy as possible and to give you the best chance of success in your AAT assessments.

They contain a number of features to help you in the study process.

The sections on the Unit Guide, the Assessment and Study Skills should be read before you commence your studies.

They are designed to familiarise you with the nature and content of the assessment and to give you tips on how best to approach your studies.

STUDY TEXT

This study text has been specially prepared for the revised AAT qualification introduced in 2013.

It is written in a practical and interactive style:

- key terms and concepts are clearly defined

- all topics are illustrated with practical examples with clearly worked solutions based on sample tasks provided by the AAT in the new examining style

- frequent activities throughout the chapters ensure that what you have learnt is regularly reinforced

- 'pitfalls' and 'examination tips' help you avoid commonly made mistakes and help you focus on what is required to perform well in your examination

- practice workbook activities can be completed at the end of each chapter.

WORKBOOK

The workbook comprises:

Practice activities at the end of each chapter with solutions at the end of the text, to reinforce the work covered in each chapter.

The questions are divided into their relevant chapters and students may either attempt these questions as they work through the textbook, or leave some or all of these until they have completed the textbook as a final revision of what they have studied.

ICONS

The study chapters include the following icons throughout.

They are designed to assist you in your studies by identifying key definitions and the points at which you can test yourself on the knowledge gained.

 Definition

These sections explain important areas of knowledge which must be understood and reproduced in an assessment

 Example

The illustrative examples can be used to help develop an understanding of topics before attempting the activity exercises

 Activity

These are exercises which give the opportunity to assess your understanding of all the assessment areas.

UNIT GUIDE

This is a level 3 unit dealing with the preparation of financial statements for sole traders and partnerships, incorporating elements of dealing with incomplete records and an appropriate understanding of the accounting requirements that underpin the preparation of financial statements.

It integrates with a number of other units in the qualification, all concerned with financial accounting. The unit builds on skills and knowledge in the two level 2 units Processing Bookkeeping Transactions (PBKT) and Control Accounts, Journals and the Banking Systems (CJBS) and the Level 3 unit Accounts Preparation (ACPR). After completion of ACPR and FSTP, the student will be ready to start developing skills and knowledge for the level 4 unit Financial Statements (FSTM). The two Level 3 units ACPR and FSTP form a bridge between Level 2 basic bookkeeping and Level 4 higher level financial accounting skills. Together, they cover the theoretical foundations of financial accounting, together with practical skills for the preparation of financial statements for unincorporated traders.

It is recommended that this unit is taken with, or after, ACPR. Both of these units are derived from the NOS FA-4, Prepare Accounts.

Purpose of the units

FSTP is the second of two Level 3 financial accounting units. The general purpose of the unit is to develop previously acquired double-entry skills and knowledge and apply these to the preparation of financial statements for sole traders and partnerships. Successful candidates will be able to identify relevant information and select appropriate skills to complete tasks and procedures and evaluate the results.

A business organisation will benefit from the provision of numerate staff able to understand the need for, and the process involved in the preparation of financial statements. Employing a student who has been successful at both Level 3 financial accounting units should result in a very useful member of the accounting team. Working with little supervision, this student should be skilled at incomplete records techniques and be capable of preparing draft financial statements for unincorporated traders.

Terminology

Students should be familiar with IFRS terminology. Other terms are used in this document to match titles in the QCF unit.

Learning objectives

After completing this unit, the student will have a good understanding of the procedures involved in, and the reasons for, preparing financial statements. This will include an awareness of the accounting systems that a business should put in place in order to produce meaningful information at the end of an accounting period. They should also develop an understanding of the environment and principles within which business operates.

The student will be introduced to the legal requirements underpinning the preparation of partnership accounting records. They will be able to prepare financial statements for a partnership showing the division of profits (or losses) after adjusting for interest on capital, interest on drawings and any salary due to each partner.

Learning outcomes and assessment criteria

The unit consists of six learning outcomes, two for Knowledge and three for Skills, with one outcome comprising a combination of Knowledge and Skills. The learning outcomes are further broken down into Assessment criteria. These are set out in the following table with Learning Outcomes in bold type and Assessment criteria listed underneath each Learning Outcome. Reference is also made to the relevant chapter within the text.

The unit consists of six learning outcomes. The learner will be able to:

1   Understand the need for, and the process involved in, the preparation of final accounts.

2   Prepare accounting records from incomplete information.

3   Produce final accounts for sole traders.

4   Understand the legislative and accounting requirements for partnerships.

5   Prepare a statement of profit or loss appropriation account.

6   Prepare a statement of financial position relating to a partnership.

There are a number of assessment criteria linked to each learning outcome. Those referenced K relate to knowledge and those referenced S relate to skills.

KAPLAN PUBLISHING

Knowledge and Skills

To perform this unit effectively you will need to know and understand the following:

Chapter

1 **Understand the need for, and the process involved in, the preparation of final accounts**

1.1K Identify reasons for closing off accounts and producing a trial balance   1,3

- Checking the accuracy of double entry.

- Providing a starting point for the preparation of financial statements.

- Clearing revenue and expense accounts for the start of the accounting period.

1.2K Explain the process, and limitations, of preparing a set of final accounts from a trial balance   1,3

- The trial balance does not prove the accuracy of records as not all errors affect the trial balance.

- The trail balance does not give a profit figure.

- The trial balance has to be sorted into statement of profit or loss and statement of financial position groupings.

- Closing inventory has to be recognised in both statement of profit or loss and statement of financial position, even if the trial balance includes a cost of goods sold account.

		Chapter
1.3K	Describe the methods of constructing accounts from incomplete records	3

- Use of control accounts

- Use of mark-up and gross sales margin

- Manipulation of figures in familiar relationships in order to find a missing figure:

  - Using the accounting equation

  - Using elements of cost of goods sold

  - Using net sales or purchases + VAT = gross

- Students may be asked to choose the most appropriate method from a list of potential ways to provide a missing figure.

1.4K	Provide reasons for imbalances resulting from incorrect double entries	3

- One-sided entries.

- Entry duplicated on one side, nothing on the other.

- Unequal entries.

- Account balance incorrectly transferred to trial balance.

- An extract from a trial balance may be provided requiring evaluation by the student, for example, providing a possible reason for a trial balance that is not balancing.

KAPLAN PUBLISHING

Chapter

1.5K	Explain reasons for incomplete records arising from insufficient data and inconsistencies with the data provided	3

- Loss of data as a result of disaster, theft or loss of books or ledgers, including records held on computer.

- Inadequate or missing records (for example, concerning receivables, purchases)

- Differences between:

   - Physical non-current assets, ledger balances, non-current asset register

   - Physical inventory count and inventory records, book figure

   - Cash book and bank statement

   - Purchase ledger balances and supplier statements

- Recognition of timing differences arising with goods or payment in transit.

2   Prepare accounting records from incomplete information

2.1S	Calculate opening and/or closing capital using incomplete information	3

- Opening and/or closing balances on asset and liability accounts may be given.

- Application of the accounting equation may be required.

- Ledger accounts or calculations may be required.

- Students may be expected to evaluate their calculations by providing a possible explanation for their results.

Chapter

2.2S   Calculate the opening and/or closing cash/bank   3
account balance

- A summary of balances or transactions may be given from which the opening or closing balance must be calculated or placed in the relevant ledger account.

- Completion of a ledger account may be required.

- An understanding that a bank statement balance 'in credit' is a debit balance in the records of the business and an overdrawn balance is a credit balance in the records of the business.

2.3S   Prepare sales and purchase ledger control   3
accounts, using these to correctly calculate sales,
purchases and the bank figures

- Incomplete information will be given. This may include, for example, opening/closing balances, bank, receipts and payments, settlement discounts, irrecoverable debts and returns

- Information may be given in the form of day-books; these may include VAT information that must be dealt with correctly in control accounts (sales, purchases, VAT).

- Some irrelevant data may be supplied; students will need to identify what is relevant

- Missing figures may include, for example, discounts, returns, irrecoverable debts, cash/credit sales and purchases, VAT, drawings.

- Completion of ledger accounts will be required.

Chapter

2.4S   Calculate account balances using mark-ups and   3
        margins

- Mark-up/gross sales margin will be given as a percentage or a fraction.

- May need to find sales, purchases, opening or closing inventory, drawings of goods.

- May need to manipulate the 'opening inventory + purchases – closing inventory = cost of goods sold' relationship to find missing figures

- May need to add/extract VAT from figures provided, or derived. Simple calculations only.

- Students should be prepared to exercise judgement in deciding whether a given figure is reasonable in the context of the data provided.

- Students may be expected to evaluate their calculations by providing a possible explanation for their results

3   Produce final accounts for sole traders

3.1K   Describe the components of a set of final accounts   1,3
        for a sole trader

- Statement of profit or loss and statement of financial position.

- Awareness of differences between these and the equivalent components for a partnership, for example the 'capital' section of the statement of financial position.

Chapter

3.2S   Prepare a statement of profit or loss   1,3

- From a balancing adjusted trial balance

- An outline pro-forma will be given, suitable for a sole trader

- May require accounts to be combined before completing pro-forma (for example, sales and sales returns) in accordance with organisational policies that will be given.

- May include balances on accounts that are dealt with in ACPR, such as non-current asset disposals, depreciation charges, irrecoverable debts, for example.

- Understand that trial balance accounts may need translation into the pro-forma names provided (for example, interest paid may need to be shown as finance costs).

- Be aware that the trial balance may include either cost of goods sold and one closing inventory entry OR two closing inventory entries, for statement of financial position and statement of profit or loss.

- Accounts such as discounts received, interest received should be treated as income that is added to gross profit, rather than shown as a 'negative expense'.

3.3S   Prepare a statement of financial position   1,3

- From a given balancing adjusted trial balance.

- An outline pro-forma will be given.

- May require accounts to be combined before completing pro-forma (for example cash + bank = cash and cash equivalents.

- Understand that the trial balance accounts may need translation into the pro-forma names provided (for example purchase ledger control account needs to be shown as trade payables).

- May include balances on accounts that are dealt with in ACPR, such as non-current assets, accumulated depreciation, allowance for doubtful debts (should be deducted from sales ledge control account to give trade receivables), accrual, for example.

- Understand that the trial balance may include accounts such as VAT, loans, bank which can appear on either side of the trial balance, and treat such balances correctly in the pro-forma.

- Basic understanding of what the capital balance for a sole trader represents and why it may increase or decrease during a period.

- Basic understanding and/or calculation of single elements from the statement of financial position specifically for a sole trader – for example, capital, drawings.

4	**Understand the legislative and accounting requirements for partnerships**	
4.1K	Describe the key components of a partnership agreement	2

- Understand what a partnership is.

- Basic description only of what is typically included and not included in the partnership agreement.

- The student should be aware of the existence and purpose of the Partnership Act 1890.

Appreciate that a formal partnership agreement may not exist for all partnerships. Relevant details of the partnership will be given, so the default provisions of the Partnership Act 1890 will not need to be recalled.

Chapter

4.2K	Describe these key components of partnership accounts	2

- Partnership appropriation account.

- Goodwill.

- Partners' current accounts.

- Partners' capital accounts.

- Statement of financial position.

5   **Prepare a statement of profit or loss appropriation account**

The following points apply to assessment criteria 5.1, 5.2 and 5.3

- Number of partners is limited to a maximum of three.

- Maximum of one change in the partnership during a period.

- Where goodwill arises, it will always be introduced and then subsequently eliminated.

- No limited liability partnerships.

- Formation of a partnership from a sole trader will not be tested.

Dissolution of a partnership will not be tested.

5.1S	Prepare the statement of profit or loss appropriation account for a partnership	2

- This will be referred to as the appropriation account.

Chapter

2

5.2S   Accurately determine the allocation of profit to partners after allowing for interest on capital, interest on drawings and any salary paid to partner(s).

The following points apply to assessment criteria 5.1 and 5.2.

- May be required to allocate a profit or a loss.

- The profit/loss for the year will be given.

- All relevant partnership agreement information will be given.

- The profit sharing ratio may be expressed as a ratio, fraction or percentage.

- A pro-forma appropriation account will be given if a full appropriation account is required.

- Alternatives to a full appropriation account may be required, for example calculations relating to the appropriations of one partner only.

- May involve change in profit share during the period. Profit will not necessarily accrue evenly over the period – the method of accrual will be given.

- Interest on capital may need to be calculated according to given information.

- Interest on drawings will not need to be calculated.

- Understand that partners' salaries are an appropriation of profit and not an expense in the statement of profit or loss.

Chapter

2

5.3S   Prepare the capital and current accounts for each partner

Current accounts

- Ledger accounts maybe required

- May include interest on capital, interest on drawings, drawings, salary and share of profit or loss

- Drawings from bank, cash or bank (ignoring VAT)

- Data may be given in the form of a completed appropriation account

- Interest on capital may need to be calculated

- Interest on drawings will not need to be calculated

- The correct entries for closure on the retirement of a partner may be required.

Capital accounts:

- Ledger accounts may be required

- May be tested in the form of opposite entries to goodwill account – accounting entries for the introduction and/or elimination of goodwill in the capital account and/or goodwill accounts may be required.

- Simple calculations relating to estimated goodwill in a business at the point of partnership change may be required

- May include calculations and accounting entries for goodwill introduced and eliminated on admission or retirement of one partner or change on profit sharing ratios of existing partners

- Appreciate that goodwill will not appear in the statement of financial position as it will always be introduced and subsequently eliminated in this assessment.

Chapter

- Capital injection will be in the form of cash/bank

- Settlement on retirement will be in the form of cash/bank or loan

- The correct entries for the admission or retirement of a partner may be required, or the injection of new capital by existing partners

- Revaluation of non-current assets will not be tested.

- Depreciation charges account.

6   Prepare a statement of financial position relating to a partnership

| 6.1S | Calculate the closing balances on each partner's capital and current accounts, including drawings | 3 |

- Drawings should be included in the current account.

| 6.2S | Prepare a statement of financial position, in compliance with the partnership agreement | 3 |

- A balancing adjusted trial balance will be given.

- The profit or loss of the period will be given. This will need to be transferred to the partners' current accounts in accordance with a given profit sharing ratio expressed as a ratio, fraction or percentage.

- An outline pro-forma will be given.

- May require accounts to be combined before completing pro-forma (for example, cash + bank = cash and cash equivalents).

- Understand that trial balance accounts may need translation into the pro-forma names provided (for example, purchase ledger control account to be shown as trade payables)

- May include balances on accounts that are dealt with in ACPR, such as non-current assets, accumulated depreciation, allowance for doubtful debts (should be deducted from sales ledger control account to give trade receivables, accruals, for example).

- Understand that the trial balance may include accounts such as VAT, loans, bank which can appear on either side of the trial balance, and treat such items correctly in the pro-forma.

THE ASSESSMENT

The format of the assessment

The assessment will consist of one section containing five independent tasks in one section. The assessment will cover:

The process of preparing financial statements, and incomplete records

A variety of techniques for finding missing figures will be required, including a selection from:

- Using the accounting equation.

- Using mark–up or gross sales margin.

- Reconstructing the capital account.

- Reconstructing the bank account.

- Reconstructing control accounts – purchases, sales, sales tax.

- Short answer questions to test the knowledge assessment criteria.

Producing financial statements for a sole trader

Typical tasks will include:

- Preparing a statement of profit or loss from a trial balance.

- Preparing a statement of financial position from a final trial balance.

- Short answer questions to test the knowledge assessment criteria.

Understanding the accounting requirements for partnerships and preparing financial statements for partnerships

Typical tasks will include:

- Preparing ledger accounts or making calculations to deal with specialised partnership transactions such as admission or retirement of a partner.

- Preparing a partnership appropriation account or partners' current accounts.

- Calculating appropriations of profit for a single partner for a given period.

- Preparing a statement of financial position from a trial balance.

- Preparing partners' capital accounts and/or a goodwill account.

- Short answer questions to test the knowledge assessment criteria.

Summary

Achievement at Level 3 reflects the ability to identify and use relevant understanding, methods and skills to complete tasks and address problems that, while well defined, have a measure of complexity. It includes taking responsibility for initiating and completing tasks and procedures as well as exercising autonomy and judgement within limited parameters. It also reflects awareness of different perspectives or approaches within an area of study or work.

Knowledge and understanding

- Use factual, procedural and theoretical understanding to complete tasks and address problems that, while well defined, may be complex and non-routine.

- Interpret and evaluate relevant information and ideas.

- Be aware of the nature of the area of study or work.

- Have awareness of different perspectives or approaches within the area of study or work.

Application and action

- Address problems that, while well defined, may be complex and non-routine.

- Identify, select and use appropriate skills, methods and procedures.

- Use appropriate investigation to inform actions.

- Review how effective methods and actions have been.

Autonomy and accountability

- Take responsibility for initiating and completing tasks and procedures, including, where relevant, responsibility for supervising or guiding others.

- Exercise autonomy and judgement within limited parameters.

Tasks types will include:

- Calculations.

- Completion of ledger accounts.

- Completion of pro-forma tables.

- non-current assets register.

- Multiple choice or similar.

Learners will normally be assessed by computer based assessment (CBA), the competency level for the AAT assessment is set at 70%.

Time allowed

The time allowed for this assessment is **two hours.**

STUDY SKILLS

Preparing to study

Devise a study plan

Determine which times of the week you will study.

Split these times into sessions of at least one hour for study of new material. Any shorter periods could be used for revision or practice.

Put the times you plan to study onto a study plan for the weeks from now until the assessment and set yourself targets for each period of study – in your sessions make sure you cover the whole course, activities and the associated questions in the workbook at the back of the manual.

If you are studying more than one unit at a time, try to vary your subjects as this can help to keep you interested and see subjects as part of wider knowledge.

When working through your course, compare your progress with your plan and, if necessary, re-plan your work (perhaps including extra sessions) or, if you are ahead, do some extra revision/practice questions.

Effective studying

Active reading

You are not expected to learn the text by rote, rather, you must understand what you are reading and be able to use it to pass the assessment and develop good practice.

A good technique is to use SQ3Rs – Survey, Question, Read, Recall, Review:

1   **Survey the chapter**

    Look at the headings and read the introduction, knowledge, skills and content, so as to get an overview of what the chapter deals with.

2   **Question**

    Whilst undertaking the survey ask yourself the questions you hope the chapter will answer for you.

3   Read

Read through the chapter thoroughly working through the activities and, at the end, making sure that you can meet the learning objectives highlighted on the first page.

4   Recall

At the end of each section and at the end of the chapter, try to recall the main ideas of the section/chapter without referring to the text. This is best done after short break of a couple of minutes after the reading stage.

5   Review

Check that your recall notes are correct.

You may also find it helpful to re-read the chapter to try and see the topic(s) it deals with as a whole.

Note taking

Taking notes is a useful way of learning, but do not simply copy out the text.

The notes must:

- be in your own words
- be concise
- cover the key points
- well organised
- be modified as you study further chapters in this text or in related ones.

Trying to summarise a chapter without referring to the text can be a useful way of determining which areas you know and which you don't.

Three ways of taking notes

1   Summarise the key points of a chapter

2   Make linear notes

A list of headings, subdivided with sub-headings listing the key points.

If you use linear notes, you can use different colours to highlight key points and keep topic areas together.

Use plenty of space to make your notes easy to use.

3   Try a diagrammatic form

The most common of which is a mind map.

To make a mind map, put the main heading in the centre of the paper and put a circle around it.

Draw lines radiating from this to the main sub-headings which again have circles around them.

Continue the process from the sub-headings to sub-sub-headings.

Highlighting and underlining

You may find it useful to underline or highlight key points in your study text – but do be selective.

You may also wish to make notes in the margins.

Revision phase

Kaplan has produced material specifically designed for your final examination preparation for this unit.

These include pocket revision notes and a bank of revision questions specifically in the style of the new syllabus.

Further guidance on how to approach the final stage of your studies is given in these materials.

Further reading

In addition to this text, you should also read the "Student section" of the "Accounting Technician" magazine every month to keep abreast of any guidance from the examiners.

KAPLAN PUBLISHING

TERMINOLOGY IAS AND UK GAAP

As of 1 January 2012 AAT will solely examine terminology consistent with IFRS and will no longer examine UK GAAP specific terminology.

The list shown gives the 'translation' between UK GAAP and IFRS. Although this is not a comprehensive list, it does cover the main terms that you will come across in your studies and assessments.

UK GAAP	IFRS
Final accounts	Financial statements
Trading and profit and loss account	Statement of profit or loss
Turnover or Sales	Revenue or Sales revenue
Interest payable	Finance costs
Bad debt expense	Irrecoverable debt expense
Operating profit	Profit from operations
Net profit/loss	Profit/Loss for the year/period
Balance sheet	Statement of financial position
Fixed assets	Non-current assets
Net book value	Carrying amount
Tangible assets	Property, plant and equipment
Reducing balance depreciation	Diminishing balance depreciation
Depreciation/Depreciation expense(s)	Depreciation charge(s)
Stocks	Inventories
Trade debtors or Debtors	Trade receivables or Receivables
Debtors ledger control account	Receivables ledger control account
Sales ledger control account	Sales ledger control account
Provision for doubtful debts	Allowance for doubtful debts
Debtors and prepayments	Trade and other receivables
Cash at bank and in hand	Cash and cash equivalents
Trade creditors or Creditors	Trade payables or Payables
Creditors ledger control account	Payables ledger control account
Purchase ledger control account	Purchase ledger control account
Creditors and accruals	Trade and other payables
Long-term liabilities	Non-current liabilities
Profit and loss balance	Retained earnings
VAT/Sales tax	VAT/Sales tax

Preparation of accounts for a sole trader

1

Introduction

For Prepare Final Accounts for Sole Traders and Partnerships you need to be able to prepare the financial statements; a statement of profit or loss and a statement of financial position for a sole trader.

These financial statements may be prepared directly from the extended trial balance or from a trial balance plus various adjustments.

In this chapter we will consider the step by step approach to the financial statements preparation, firstly from an extended trial balance and then directly from an initial trial balance.

The knowledge for this unit has been acquired in Accounts Preparation but within this unit, you will be expected to apply the skills to complete the financial statements.

KNOWLEDGE

Identify reasons for closing off accounts and producing a trial balance (1.1)

Explain the process, and limitations, of preparing a set of final accounts from a trial balance (1.2)

Describe the components of a set of final accounts for a sole trader (3.1)

SKILLS

Prepare a statement of profit or loss (3.2)

Prepare a statement of financial position (3.3)

CONTENTS

1 Statement of profit or loss for a sole trader
2 The statement of financial position for a sole trader
3 Preparing financial statements from the trial balance
4 Summary

1 Statement of profit or loss for a sole trader

1.1 Introduction

In Accounts Preparation we considered in outline the layout of a statement of profit or loss for a sole trader. Now we will consider it in more detail.

1.2 Statement of profit or loss

Technically the statement of profit or loss is split into two elements:

- the trading account to determine gross profit;
- the statement of profit or loss to determine net profit.

However, in general the whole statement is referred to as the statement of profit or loss.

1.3 Trading account

The trading account calculates the gross profit or loss that has been made from the trading activities of the sole trader – the buying and selling of goods.

 Definition

The gross profit (or loss) is the profit (or loss) from the trading activities of the sole trader.

The trading account looks like this:

	£	£
Revenue		X
Less: Cost of sales		
Opening inventory	X	
Purchases	X	
	―	
	X	
Less: Closing inventory	(X)	
	―	(X)
Gross profit (loss)		X
		―

1.4 Profit or loss

The remaining content of the statement of profit or loss is a list of the expenses of the business. These are deducted from the gross profit to give the profit for the year (or the net profit).

Definition

The net profit or loss is the profit or loss after deduction of all of the expenses of the business.

Activity 1

Statement of profit or loss for the year ended 31 December 20X2.

Calculate the revenue and cost of sales (complete the boxes).

	£	£
Revenue		
Less: Cost of sales		
Opening inventory	37,500	
Purchases	158,700	
	196,200	
Less: Closing inventory	(15,000)	
Gross profit		111,300

A typical statement of profit or loss is shown below.

Statement of profit or loss of Stanley for the year-ended 31 December 20X2

	£	£
Revenue		X
Less: Cost of sales		
Inventory on 1 January (opening inventory)	X	
Add: Purchases of goods	X	
	–––	
	X	
Less: Inventory on 31 December (closing inventory)	(X)	
	–––	(X)
		–––
Gross profit		X
Sundry income:		
Discounts received	X	
Commission received	X	
Rent received	X	
	–––	X
		–––
		X
Less: Expenses:		
Rent	X	
Rates	X	
Lighting and heating	X	
Telephone	X	
Postage	X	
Insurance	X	
Stationery	X	
Payroll expenses	X	
Depreciation	X	
Accountancy and audit fees	X	
Bank charges and interest	X	
Irrecoverable debts	X	
Allowance for doubtful debts adjustment	X	
Delivery costs	X	
Van running expenses	X	
Selling expenses	X	
Discounts allowed	X	
	–––	(X)
		–––
Profit/(loss) for the year		X/(X)
		–––

1.5 Preparation of the statement of profit or loss

The statement of profit or loss is prepared by listing all of the entries from the ETB that are in the profit or loss columns.

 Example

Given below is the final ETB for Lyttleton

Account name	Trial balance		Adjustments		Profit or loss statement		Statement of fin. pos.	
	Dr £	Cr £	Dr £	Cr £	Dr £	Cr £	Dr £	Cr £
Capital		7,830						7,830
Cash	2,010						2,010	
Non-current assets	9,420						9,420	
Accumulated depreciation		3,470		942				4,412
SLCA	1,830						1,830	
Open. inventory	1,680				1,680			
PLCA		390						390
Sales		14,420				14,420		
Purchases	8,180			1,500	6,680			
Rent	1,100		100		1,200			
Electricity	940		400		1,340			
Rates	950			200	750			
Depreciation expense			942		942			
Allowance for doubtful debts adjustments			55		55			
Allowance for doubtful debts				55				55
Drawings			1,500				1,500	
Accruals				500				500
Prepayments			200				200	
Closing inventory SoFP			1,140				1,140	
Closing inventory I/S				1,140		1,140		
Profit					2,913			2,913
	26,110	26,110	4,337	4,337	15,560	15,560	16,100	16,100

We will now show how the final statement of profit or loss for Lyttleton would look.

Solution

Statement of profit or loss of Lyttleton for the year-ended 31 December 20X5

		£	£
Revenue			14,420
Less:	Cost of sales		
	Opening inventory	1,680	
	Purchases	6,680	
		———	
		8,360	
Less:	Closing inventory	(1,140)	
		———	
			(7,220)
			———
Gross profit			7,200
Less: Expenses			
	Rent	1,200	
	Electricity	1,340	
	Rates	750	
	Depreciation	942	
	Allowance for doubtful debts increase	55	
		———	
Total expenses			(4,287)
			———
Net profit for the year			2,913
			———

All of the figures in the statement of profit or loss columns in the ETB have been used to prepare this statement of profit or loss.

The final net profit is the profit figure calculated as a balancing figure in the ETB.

2 The statement of financial position for a sole trader

2.1 Introduction

We have considered the statement of financial position in outline in the Accounts Preparation unit and now we will consider it in more detail.

> **Definition**
>
> A statement of financial position is a list of the assets and liabilities of the sole trader at the end of the accounting period.

The assets are split into non-current assets and current assets.

> **Definition**
>
> Non-current assets are assets that will be used within the business over a long period (usually greater than one year), e.g. land and buildings

> **Definition**
>
> Current assets are assets that are expected to be realised within the business in the normal course of trading (usually a period less than one year) e.g. inventory.

The liabilities are split into current liabilities and non-current liabilities.

> **Definition**
>
> Current liabilities are the short term payables of a business. This generally means payables that are due to be paid within twelve months of the statement of financial position date e.g. trade payables

> **Definition**
>
> Non-current liabilities are payables that will be paid over a longer period, which is normally in excess of one year, e.g. loans

Preparation of accounts for a sole trader: **Chapter 1**

An example of a typical sole trader's statement of financial position is given below:

Statement of financial position of Stanley at 31 December 20X2

	Cost £	Depreciation £	£
Non-current assets			
Freehold factory	X	X	X
Machinery	X	X	X
Motor vehicles	X	X	X
	X	X	X
Current assets			
Inventories		X	
Trade receivables	X		
Less: Allowance for doubtful debts	(X)		
		X	
Prepayments		X	
Cash at bank		X	
Cash in hand		X	
		X	
Current liabilities			
Trade payables	X		
Accruals	X		
		(X)	
Net current assets			X
Total assets less current liabilities			X
Non-current liabilities			
12% loan			(X)
Net assets			X
Capital at 1 January			X
Net profit for the year			X
			X
Less: Drawings			(X)
Proprietor's funds			X

2.2 Assets and liabilities

The assets and liabilities in a formal statement of financial position are listed in a particular order:

- firstly the non-current assets less the accumulated depreciation (remember that this net total is known as the carrying value)

- next the current assets in the following order – inventory, receivables, prepayments then bank and cash balances

- next the current liabilities – payables and accruals that are payable within 12 months

- finally the long-term payables such as loan accounts.

The assets are all added together and the liabilities are then deducted. This gives the statement of financial position total.

2.3 Capital balances

The total of the assets less liabilities of the sole trader should be equal to the capital of the sole trader.

The capital is shown in the statement of financial position as follows:

	£
Opening capital at the start of the year	X
Add: Net profit/(loss) for the year	X
	X
Less: Drawings	(X)
Closing capital	X

This closing capital should equal the total of all of the assets less all liabilities, as shown in the accounting equation assets – liabilities = capital. (NB: this formula can be rearranged as assets = capital + liabilities).

The capital balance represents the owner's funds, i.e. what the owner will be left with if the business is wound up and all the assets are sold and all the liabilities paid off.

Example

Given below is the completed ETB for Lyttleton. This time the statement of financial position will be prepared.

Account name	Trial balance		Adjustments		Income statement		Statement of fin. pos.	
	Dr £	Cr £	Dr £	Cr £	Dr £	Cr £	Dr £	Cr £
Capital		7,830						7,830
Cash	2,010						2,010	
Non-current assets	9,420						9,420	
Accumulated depreciation		3,470		942				4,412
SLCA	1,830						1,830	
Inventory	1,680				1,680			
PLCA		390						390
Revenue		14,420				14,420		
Purchases	8,180			1,500	6,680			
Rent	1,100		100		1,200			
Electricity	940		400		1,340			
Rates	950			200	750			
Depreciation expense			942		942			
Allowance for doubtful debts adjustments			55		55			
Allowance for doubtful debts				55				55
Drawings			1,500				1,500	
Accruals				500				500
Prepayments			200				200	
Closing inventory: P&L				1,140		1,140		
Closing inventory: SoFP			1,140				1,140	
Profit (15,560 – 12,647)					2,913			2,913
	26,110	**26,110**	**4,337**	**4,337**	**15,560**	**15,560**	**16,100**	**16,100**

Each of the assets and liabilities that appear in the statement of financial position columns will appear in the statement of financial position.

Solution

Statement of financial position of Lyttleton at 31 December 20X5

	Cost	Accumulated Dep'n	
	£	£	£
Non-current assets	9,420	4,412	5,008
Current assets			
Inventories		1,140	
Trade receivables	1,830		
Less: Allowance for doubtful debts	(55)		
		1,775	
Prepayments		200	
Cash		2,010	
		5,125	
Less:			
Current liabilities			
Payables	390		
Accruals	500		
		(890)	
Net current assets			4,235
Net assets			9,243
Capital 1 January			7,830
Net profit for the year			2,913
			10,743
Less: Drawings			(1,500)
Proprietor's funds			9,243

Note

- the non-current assets are shown at their carrying value;

- the current assets are sub-totalled as are the current liabilities – the current liabilities are then deducted from the current assets to give net current assets;

- the net current assets are added to the non-current asset carrying value to reach the statement of financial position total, net assets.

The statement of financial position total of net assets should be equal to the closing capital; the statement of financial position is then said to balance (it used to be referred to as a 'balance sheet'). If your statement of financial position does not balance then make some quick checks, such as basic arithmetic and missing figures. Do not spend too much time searching for your error as the time can be better used on the rest of the examination. If you have time left over at the end then you can return to the question to look for the error.

 Activity 2

Given below is a completed extended trial balance.

Extended trial balance at 31 December 20X6

Account name	Trial balance Dr £	Trial balance Cr £	Adjustments Dr £	Adjustments Cr £	Statement of profit or loss Dr £	Statement of profit or loss Cr £	Statement of fin. pos. Dr £	Statement of fin. pos. Cr £
Fittings	7,300						7,300	
Accumulated depreciation 1.1.X6		2,500		400				2,900
Leasehold	30,000						30,000	
Accumulated depreciation 1.1.X6		6,000		1,000				7,000
Inventory 1 January 20X6	15,000				15,000			
Sales ledger control account	10,000			500			9,500	
Allowance for doubtful debts 1.1.X6		800	515					285
Cash in hand	50						50	
Cash at bank	1,250						1,250	
Purchases ledger control account		18,000						18,000
Capital		19,050						19,050
Drawings	4,750		1,200				5,950	
Purchases	80,000			1,200	78,800			
Revenue		120,000				120,000		
Wages	12,000			200	11,800			
Advertising	4,000		200		4,200			
Rates	1,800			360	1,440			
Bank charges	200				200			
Depreciation – Fittings			400		400			
Depreciation – Lease			1,000		1,000			

Allowance for doubtful debts adjustments			515		515		
Irrecoverable debts		500		500			
Prepayments		360				360	
Closing inventory SoFP		21,000				21,000	
Closing inventory P&L			21,000	21,000			
				113,340	141,515		
Net profit				28,175			28,175
	166,350	166,350	25,175	25,175	141,515	141,515	75,410	75,410

Prepare the statement of profit or loss for the business.

Pick the appropriate account heading from the options below.

Statement of profit or loss for the year-ended 31 December 20X6

	£	£
Revenue		
Less: Cost of sales		
Opening inventory/Closing inventory/Purchases		
Purchases/Opening inventory/Closing inventory		
	_____	
Opening inventory/Closing inventory/Purchases		
	_____	
		_____
Gross profit		
Less: Expenses		
Trade receivables/Wages		
Advertising/Prepayments		
Drawings/Rates		
Bank charges/Capital		
Depreciation/Accumulated depreciation – F&F		
– lease		
Allowance for doubtful debts adjustment		
Irrecoverable debts		
	_____	
Total expenses		
		_____
Profit for the year		
		_____

Prepare the statement of financial position for the business.

Pick the appropriate account heading from the options below.

Statement of financial position as at 31 December 20X6

	£	£	£
Non-current assets:			
Fittings/Closing inventory			
Trade receivables/Leasehold	_____	_____	_____
	_____	_____	
Current assets:			
Closing inventory/Opening inventory			
Trade payables/Trade receivables			
Less: Allowance for doubtful debts	_____		
Accruals/Prepayments			
Cash at bank/Drawings			
Capital/Cash in hand		_____	
Current liabilities:			
Trade receivables/Trade payables		_____	
			_____
			_____
Owner's capital			
Capital at 1.1.X6			
Drawings/Net profit for the year			_____
Less: Capital/Drawings			_____
			_____

3 Preparing financial statements from the trial balance

3.1 Introduction

As we have seen in Accounts Preparation, the extended trial balance is a useful working paper for the eventual preparation of the financial statements of a sole trader. However, in the examination you may well be required to prepare a set of financial statements directly from the trial balance.

In this section we will work through a comprehensive example which will include the extraction of the initial trial balance, correction of errors and clearing a suspense account, accounting for year-end adjustments and finally the preparation of the financial statements.

Example

Given below are the balances taken from a sole trader's ledger accounts on 31 March 20X4

	£
Sales ledger control account	30,700
Telephone	1,440
Purchases ledger control account	25,680
Heat and light	2,480
Motor vehicles at cost	53,900
Computer equipment at cost	4,500
Carriage inwards	1,840
Carriage outwards	3,280
Wages	67,440
Loan interest	300
Capital	48,000
Drawings	26,000
Allowance for doubtful debts	450
Bank overdraft	2,880
Purchases	126,800
Petty cash	50
Revenue	256,400
Insurance	3,360
Accumulated depreciation – motor vehicles	15,000
Accumulated depreciation – computer equipment	2,640
Inventory at 1 April 20X3	13,200
Loan	8,000
Rent	23,760

The following information is also available:

(i)   The value of inventory at 31 March 20X4 was £14,400.

(ii)   Motor vehicles are to be depreciated at 30% on reducing balance basis and computer equipment at 20% on cost.

(iii) A telephone bill for £180 for the three months to 31 March 20X4 did not arrive until after the trial balance had been drawn up.

(iv)   Of the insurance payments, £640 is for the year-ending 31 March 20X5.

(v)   An irrecoverable debt of £700 is to be written off and an allowance of 2% is required against the remaining receivables.

Solution

Step 1

The first stage is to draw up the initial trial balance. Remember that assets and expenses are debit balances and liabilities and income are credit balances.

	£	£
Sales ledger control account	30,700	
Telephone	1,440	
Purchases ledger control account		25,680
Heat and light	2,480	
Motor vehicles at cost	53,900	
Computer equipment at cost	4,500	
Carriage inwards	1,840	
Carriage outwards	3,280	
Wages	67,440	
Loan interest	300	
Capital		48,000
Drawings	26,000	
Allowance for doubtful debts		450
Bank overdraft		2,880
Purchases	126,800	
Petty cash	50	
Revenue		256,400
Insurance	3,360	
Accumulated depreciation – motor vehicles		15,000
Accumulated depreciation– computer equipment		2,640
Inventory at 1 April 20X3	13,200	
Loan		8,000
Rent	23,760	
	359,050	359,050

Step 2

Now to deal with the year-end adjustments:

(a)   The value of inventory at 31 March 20X4 was £14,400.

Closing inventory – profit or loss

	£		£
		Closing inventory statement of financial position	14,400

Closing inventory – statement of financial position

	£		£
Closing inventory income statement	14,400		

- We now have the closing inventory for the statement of profit or loss.

(b)   The motor vehicles and computer equipment have yet to be depreciated for the year. Motor vehicles are depreciated at 30% on reducing balance basis and computer equipment at 20% on cost.

Motor vehicles depreciation (53,900 – 15,000) × 30% = £11,670

Computer equipment depreciation 4,500 × 20% = £900

Depreciation expense account – motor vehicles

	£		£
Accumulated depreciation	11,670		

Accumulated depreciation account – motor vehicles

	£		£
		Balance b/d	15,000
Balance c/d	26,670	Depreciation expense	11,670
	26,670		26,670
		Balance b/d	26,670

Depreciation expense account – computer equipment

	£		£
Accumulated depreciation	900		

Accumulated depreciation account – computer equipment

	£		£
		Balance b/d	2,640
Balance c/d	3,540	Depreciation expense	900
	———		———
	3,540		3,540
	———		———
		Balance b/d	3,540

(c) A telephone bill for £180 for the three months to 31 March 20X4 did not arrive until after the trial balance had been drawn up.

This needs to be accrued for:

Debit	Telephone	£180
Credit	Accruals	£180

Telephone account

	£		£
Balance b/d	1,440		
Accrual	180	Balance c/d	1,620
	———		———
	1,620		1,620
	———		———
Balance b/d	1,620		

Accruals

	£		£
		Telephone	180

(d) Of the insurance payments £640 is for the year-ending 31 March 20X5.

This must be adjusted for as a prepayment:

Debit	Prepayment	£640
Credit	Insurance account	£640

Prepayments

	£		£
Insurance	640		

Insurance account

	£		£
Balance b/d	3,360	Prepayment	640
		Balance c/d	2,720
	3,360		3,360
Balance b/d	2,720		

(e) An irrecoverable debt of £700 is to be written off and an allowance of 2% is required against the remaining receivables.

Firstly, the irrecoverable debt must be written off in order to find the amended balance on the sales ledger control account.

Debit   Irrecoverable debts expense   £700

Credit   Sales ledger control account   £700

Irrecoverable debts expense account

	£		£
Sales ledger control account	700		

Sales ledger control account

	£		£
Balance b/d	30,700	Irrecoverable debts expense	700
		Balance c/d	30,000
	30,700		30,700
Balance b/d	30,000		

Now we can determine the allowance for doubtful debts required at £30,000 × 2% = £600. The balance on the allowance account in the trial balance is £450, therefore an increase of £150 is required.

Debit   Allowance for doubtful debts adjustment (P&L)   £150

Credit   Allowance for doubtful debts account (SoFP)   £150

Allowance for doubtful debts adjustment account

	£		£
Allowance for doubtful debts	150	Balance c/d	150
	────		────
	150		150
	────		────
Balance b/d	150		

Allowance for doubtful debts account

	£		£
		Balance b/d	450
Balance c/d	600	Allowance for doubtful debts adjustment	150
	────		────
	600		600
	────		────
		Balance b/d	600

Step 5

Now that all of the adjustments have been put through the ledger accounts, an amended trial balance can be drawn up as a check and as a starting point for preparing the financial statements.

Remember to consider the adjustments just identified when preparing the trial balance.

Trial balance at 31 March 20X4

	£	£
Sales ledger control account	30,000	
Telephone	1,620	
Purchases ledger control account		25,680
Heat and light	2,480	
Motor vehicles at cost	53,900	
Computer equipment at cost	4,500	
Carriage inwards	1,840	
Carriage outwards	3,280	
Wages	67,440	
Loan interest	300	
Capital		48,000
Drawings	26,000	
Allowance for doubtful debts		600
Bank overdraft		2,880
Purchases	126,800	
Petty cash	50	
Revenue		256,400
Insurance	2,720	
Accumulated depreciation – motor vehicles		26,670
Accumulated depreciation – computer equipment		3,540
Inventory at 1 April 20X3	13,200	
Loan		8,000
Rent	23,760	
Inventory at 31 March 20X4	14,400	14,400
Depreciation expense – motor vehicles	11,670	
Depreciation expense – computer equipment	900	
Accruals		180
Prepayments	640	
Allowance for doubtful debt adjustment	150	
Irrecoverable debts expense	700	
	_____	_____
	386,350	386,350
	_____	_____

Step 6

We are now in a position to prepare the financial statements for the sole trader. Take care with the carriage inwards and carriage outwards. They are both expenses of the business but carriage inwards is treated as part of cost of sales, whereas carriage outwards is one of the list of expenses.

Statement of profit or loss for the year-ended 31 March 20X4

	£	£
Revenue		256,400
Less: Cost of sales		
Opening inventory	13,200	
Carriage inwards	1,840	
Purchases	126,800	
	141,840	
Less: Closing inventory	(14,400)	
		127,440
Gross profit		128,960
Less: Expenses		
Telephone	1,620	
Heat and light	2,480	
Carriage outwards	3,280	
Wages	67,440	
Loan interest	300	
Insurance	2,720	
Rent	23,760	
Depreciation expense – motor vehicles	11,670	
Depreciation expense – computer equipment	900	
Irrecoverable debts	700	
Allowance for doubtful debts adjustment	150	
Total expenses		115,020
Profit for the year		13,940

Statement of financial position as at 31 March 20X4

	Cost	Accumulated depreciation	Carrying value
	£	£	£
Non-current assets			
Motor vehicles	53,900	26,670	27,230
Computer equipment	4,500	3,540	960
	58,400	30,210	28,190
Current assets			
Inventory		14,400	
Trade receivables	30,000		
Less: Allowance for doubtful debts	(600)		
		29,400	
Prepayment		640	
Petty cash		50	
		44,490	
Current liabilities			
Bank overdraft	2,880		
Trade Payables	25,680		
Accruals	180		
		28,740	
Net current assets			15,750
Total assets less current liabilities			43,940
Non-current liability:			
Loan			(8,000)
Net assets			35,940
Capital			
Opening capital			48,000
Net profit for the year			13,940
			61,940
Less: Drawings			26,000
Proprietor's funds			35,940

Activity 3

Given below is the list of ledger balances for a sole trader at 30 June 20X4 after all year-end adjustments have been put through.

	£
Revenue	165,400
Sales ledger control account	41,350
Wages	10,950
Bank	1,200
Rent	8,200
Capital	35,830
Purchases ledger control account	15,100
Purchases	88,900
Electricity	1,940
Telephone	980
Drawings	40,000
Inventory at 1 July 20X3	9,800
Motor vehicles at cost	14,800
Accumulated depreciation – motor vehicles	7,800
Fixtures at cost	3,200
Accumulated depreciation – fittings	1,800
Accruals	100
Prepayments	210
Inventory at 30 June 20X4 – statement of financial position	8,300
Inventory at 30 June 20X4 – profit or loss	8,300
Depreciation expense – motor vehicles	3,700
Depreciation expense – fittings	800

You are required to:

(i)   Draw up a trial balance to check that it balances (you should find that the trial balance does balance).

(ii) Prepare the financial statements for the sole trader for the year-ending 30 June 20X4.

(i) **Trial balance as at 30 June 20X4**

	£	£
Revenue		
Sales ledger control account		
Wages		
Bank		
Rent		
Capital		
Purchases ledger control account		
Purchases		
Electricity		
Telephone		
Drawings		
Inventory at 1 July 20X3		
Motor vehicles at cost		
Accumulated depreciation – motor vehicles		
Fixtures at cost		
Accumulated depreciation – fittings		
Accruals		
Prepayments		
Inventory at 30 June 20X4 – SoFP		
Inventory at 30 June 20X4 – P&L		
Depreciation expense – motor vehicles		
Depreciation expense – fittings		

(ii) **Statement of profit or loss for the year-ending 30 June 20X4**

	£	£
Revenue		
Less: Cost of sales		
	———	
Less:		
	———	
		———
Gross profit		
Less: Expenses		
	———	
Total expenses		
Net profit		———
		———

Statement of financial position as at 30 June 20X4

	Cost £	Depreciation £	CV £
Non-current assets			
	_____	_____	_____
	_____	_____	_____
Current assets			
		_____	
Current liabilities			
	_____		
		_____	
Net current assets			
			_____
Net assets			
			_____
Capital			
Net profit for the year			
			_____
Drawings			
			_____
Proprietor's funds			
			_____

Activity 4

Tick as appropriate.

1   Opening inventory is recorded in the statement of profit or loss as

An expense ☐

Cost of sales ☐

2   Indicate where the drawings should be shown in the financial statements

Profit or loss expenses ☐

Statement of financial position as a deduction to capital ☐

3   Payroll expenses are recorded as

A liability in the statement of financial position ☐

An expense in the statement of profit or loss ☐

4   Does the allowance for doubtful debt adjustment appear in the statement of profit or loss or the statement of financial position?

Statement of profit or loss ☐

Statement of financial position ☐

5   Irrecoverable debt expenses are recorded in the statement of financial position as an increase in the allowance for doubtful debts

True ☐

False ☐

4 Summary

The unit Prepare Final Accounts for Sole Traders and Partnerships requires the preparation of the financial statements for a sole trader.

The statement of profit or loss for the period summarises the transactions in the period and leads to a net profit or loss for the period.

The statement of financial position lists the assets and liabilities of the business on the last day of the accounting period in a particular order.

If you have to prepare the financial statements from an extended trial balance then each balance will already have been classified as either a profit or loss item or a statement of financial position item.

If you are preparing the financial statements from a trial balance, you will have to recognise whether the balances should appear in the statement of profit or loss or in the statement of financial position.

Answers to chapter activities

Activity 1

Statement of profit or loss extract for the year-ended 31 December 20X2

Calculate the sales and cost of sales.

	£	£
Revenue		292,500
Less: Cost of sales		
Opening inventory	37,500	
Purchases	158,700	
	196,200	
Less: Closing inventory	(15,000)	
		(181,200)
Gross profit		111,300

Activity 2

Statement of profit or loss for the year-ended 31 December 20X6

	£	£
Revenue		120,000
Less: Cost of sales		
Opening inventory	15,000	
Purchases	78,800	
	93,800	
Less: Closing inventory	(21,000)	
		(72,800)
Gross profit		47,200

Less: Expenses		
Wages	11,800	
Advertising	4,200	
Rates	1,440	
Bank charges	200	
Depreciation – F&F	400	
– lease	1,000	
Allowance for doubtful debts adjustment	(515)	
Irrecoverable debts	500	
Total expenses		(19,025)
Profit for the year		28,175

Statement of financial position at 31 December 20X6

	£	£	£
Non-current assets			
Fittings	7,300	2,900	4,400
Leasehold	30,000	7,000	23,000
	37,300	9,900	27,400
Current assets			
Inventory		21,000	
Trade receivables	9,500		
Less: Allowance for doubtful debts	(285)		
		9,215	
Prepayments		360	
Cash at bank		1,250	
Cash in hand		50	
		31,875	
Current liabilities			
Trade payables		(18,000)	
Net current assets			13,875
Net assets			41,275
Owner's capital			
Capital at 1.1.X6			19,050
Net profit for the year			28,175
Less: Drawings			(5,950)
Proprietor's funds			41,275

Activity 3

(i)   **Trial balance as at 30 June 20X4**

	£	£
Revenue		165,400
Sales ledger control account	41,350	
Wages	10,950	
Bank	1,200	
Rent	8,200	
Capital		35,830
Purchases ledger control account		15,100
Purchases	88,900	
Electricity	1,940	
Telephone	980	
Drawings	40,000	
Inventory at 1 July 20X3	9,800	
Motor vehicles at cost	14,800	
Accumulated depreciation – motor vehicles		7,800
Fixtures at cost	3,200	
Accumulated depreciation – fittings		1,800
Accruals		100
Prepayments	210	
Inventory at 30 June 20X4 – P&L		8,300
Inventory at 30 June 20X4 – SoFP	8,300	
Depreciation expense – motor vehicles	3,700	
Depreciation expense – fittings	800	
	234,330	234,330

(ii) **Statement of profit or loss for the year-ending 30 June 20X4**

	£	£
Revenue		165,400
Less: Cost of sales		
Opening inventory	9,800	
Purchases	88,900	
	98,700	
Less: Closing inventory	(8,300)	
		(90,400)
Gross profit		75,000
Less: Expenses		
Wages	10,950	
Rent	8,200	
Electricity	1,940	
Telephone	980	
Depreciation – motor vehicles	3,700	
Depreciation – fittings	800	
Total expenses		(26,570)
Net profit		48,430

Statement of financial position as at 30 June 20X4

	Cost £	Depreciation £	CV £
Non-current assets			
Motor vehicles	14,800	7,800	7,000
Fittings	3,200	1,800	1,400
	18,000	9,600	8,400
Current assets			
Inventory		8,300	
Trade receivables		41,350	
Prepayments		210	
Bank		1,200	
		51,060	
Current liabilities			
Trade payables	15,100		
Accruals	100		
		(15,200)	
Net current assets			35,860
Net assets			44,260
Capital			35,830
Net profit for the year			48,430
			84,260
Drawings			(40,000)
Proprietor's funds			44,260

KAPLAN PUBLISHING

Activity 4

1   Opening inventory is recorded in the statement of profit or loss as

Cost of sales

2   Indicate where the drawings should be shown in the financial statements

Statement of financial position

3   Payroll expenses are recorded as

An expense in the statement of profit or loss

4   Does the allowance for doubtful debt adjustment appear in the statement of profit or loss or statement of financial position?

Statement of profit or loss

5   Irrecoverable debt expenses are recorded in the statement of financial position as an increase in the allowance for doubtful debts

False

5 Test your knowledge

 Workbook Activity 5

David Pedley

The following information is available for David Pedley's business for the year-ended 31 December 20X8. He started his business on 1 January 20X8.

	£
Payables	6,400
Receivables	5,060
Purchases	16,100
Revenue	28,400
Motor van	1,700
Drawings	5,100
Insurance	174
General expenses	1,596
Rent and rates	2,130
Salaries	4,162
Inventory at 31 December 20X8	2,050
Sales returns	200
Cash at bank	2,628
Cash in hand	50
Capital introduced	4,100

Required:

Prepare a statement of profit or loss for the year-ended 31 December 20X8 and a statement of financial position at that date.

Workbook Activity 6

Karen Finch

On 1 April 20X7 Karen Finch started a business with capital of £10,000 which she paid into a business bank account.

The following is a summary of the cash transactions for the first year.

	£
Amounts received from customers	17,314
Salary of assistant	2,000
Cash paid to suppliers for purchases	10,350
Purchase of motor van on 31 March 20X8	4,000
Drawings during the year	2,400
Amounts paid for electricity	560
Rent and rates for one year	1,100
Postage and stationery	350

At the end of the year, Karen was owed £4,256 by her customers and owed £5,672 to her suppliers. She has promised her assistant a bonus for the year of £400. At 31 March 20X8 this had not been paid.

At 31 March 20X8 there was closing inventory of £4,257 and the business owed £170 for electricity for the last quarter of the year. A year's depreciation is to be charged on the motor van at 25% on cost.

Required:

Prepare a statement of profit or loss for the year-ended 31 March 20X8 and a statement of financial position at that date.

Workbook Activity 7

The trial balance of Elmdale at 31 December 20X8 is as follows

	Dr £	Cr £
Capital		8,602
Inventory	2,700	
Revenue		21,417
Purchases	9,856	
Rates	1,490	
Drawings	4,206	
Electricity	379	
Freehold shop	7,605	
Receivables	2,742	
Payables		3,617
Cash at bank		1,212
Cash in hand	66	
Sundry expenses	2,100	
Wages and salaries	3,704	
	34,848	34,848

In addition, Elmdale provides the following information:

(i) Closing inventory has been valued for accounts purposes at £3,060.

(ii) An electricity bill amounting to £132 in respect of the quarter to 28 February 20X9 was paid on 7 March 20X9.

(iii) Rates include a payment of £1,260 made on 10 April 20X8 in respect of the year to 31 March 20X9.

Tasks

(a) Show the adjustments to the ledger accounts for the end-of-period adjustments (i) to (iii).

(b) Prepare a statement of profit or loss for the year-ended 31 December 20X8.

Partnership accounts

2

Introduction

For Prepare Final Accounts for Sole Traders and Partnerships you need to apply acquired knowledge and skills from Accounts Preparation (ACPR) to prepare a set of partnership accounts.

You need to be able to prepare a statement of profit or loss for a partnership, which is no different to that for a sole trader, then prepare a partnership appropriation account and a statement of financial position for the partnership.

You also need to be able to deal with events such as the admission of a new partner or the retirement of a partner.

All of this will be dealt with in this chapter.

KNOWLEDGE

Describe the key components of a partnership agreement, including partnership appropriation account, goodwill, partners' capital and current accounts, and statement of financial position (4.1), (4.2)

SKILLS

Prepare the statement of profit or loss appropriation account for a partnership (5.1)

Accurately determine the allocation of profit to partners after allowing for interest on capital and drawings and any salary paid to partner(s) (5.2)

Prepare the capital and current accounts for each partner, including drawings and calculation of closing balances(5.3), (6.1)

Prepare a partnership statement of financial position (6.2)

CONTENTS

1 Accounting for partner's capital and profits
2 Appropriation of profit
3 Changes in the partnership agreement
4 Admission of a new partner
5 Retirement of a partner
6 Preparing financial statements for a partnership
7 Summary

1 Accounting for partner's capital and profits

1.1   What is a partnership?

 Definition

A partnership is where two or more people carry on business together with a view to making a profit and sharing that profit.

In a partnership each of the partners will introduce capital into the business and each partner will have a share in the profits of the business.

1.2   Partnership capital

Each of the partners in a partnership will invest capital into the business in just the same way that a sole trader does.

In a partnership accounting system it is important to keep the capital paid in by each partner separate so that there is a record of how much the business owes back to each of the partners.

In order to keep a record of the capital invested by each partner a separate capital account for each partner is kept in the general ledger.

 Definition

A capital account in a partnership is an account for each partner which records the capital that they have invested into the business.

When a partner invests capital into the business the double entry is:

Dr   Bank account

Cr   Partner's capital account

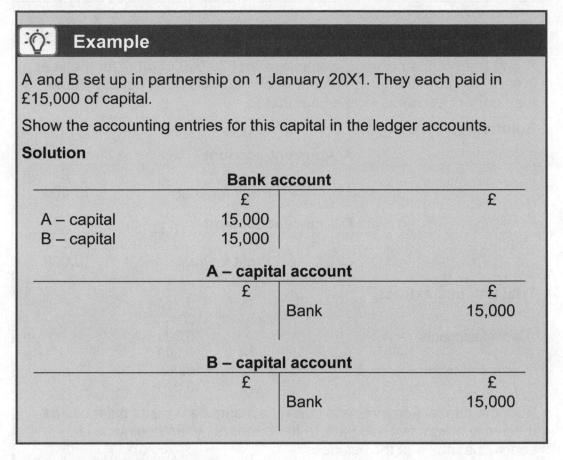

Example

A and B set up in partnership on 1 January 20X1. They each paid in £15,000 of capital.

Show the accounting entries for this capital in the ledger accounts.

Solution

Bank account

	£		£
A – capital	15,000		
B – capital	15,000		

A – capital account

	£		£
		Bank	15,000

B – capital account

	£		£
		Bank	15,000

1.3 Partnership profits

When a partnership makes a profit or a loss for an accounting period then this must be shared between the partners.

Usually there will be a partnership agreement which sets out what percentage of the profit each partner is to receive.

If there is no written partnership agreement then the Partnership Act 1890 states that profits should be shared equally between all of the partners.

1.4 Accounting for partnership profits

The profit that each partner is due from the business is recorded in individual current accounts.

Definition

The partners' current accounts record the amount of profit that is due to each partner from the business. This is not to be confused with the bank account of the same name.

Example

A and B, from the previous example, earn £20,000 of profit for the year 20X1. The partnership agreement is to share this profit equally. Show their current accounts for the year 20X1.

Solution

A – current account

	£			£
			Profit for year	10,000

B – current account

	£			£
			Profit for year	10,000

Trial balance extract

		Dr	Cr
Capital accounts	– A		15,000
	– B		15,000
Current accounts	– A		10,000
	– B		10,000

Both the capital accounts and current accounts are credit balances as these are amounts owed back to the partners by the business, i.e. special payables of the business.

The credit balance in the partners' current accounts is the same as the credit balance for 'net profit for the year' on the bottom half of the sole trader statement of financial position. It represents the funds due to the proprietors.

1.5 Drawings

Just as a sole trader takes money and/or goods out of the business, then partners will do exactly the same thing. If a partner withdraws cash the double entry would be:

Dr Partner's current account
Cr Bank account

If they withdraw inventory the double entry would be:

Dr Partner's current account
Cr Purchases

KAPLAN PUBLISHING

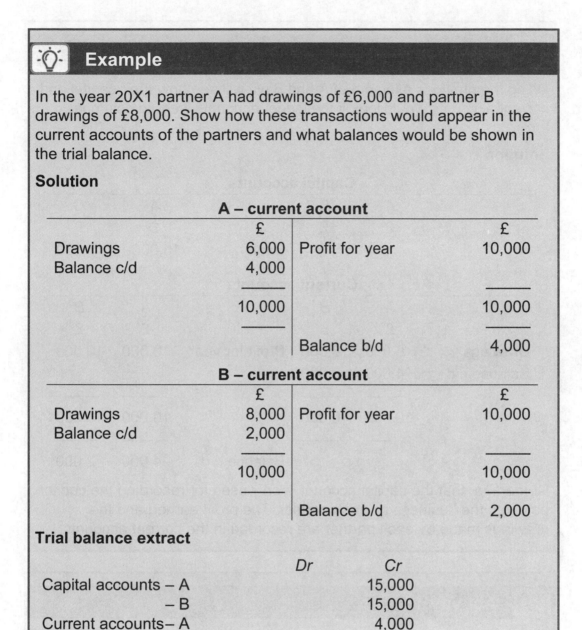

Example

In the year 20X1 partner A had drawings of £6,000 and partner B drawings of £8,000. Show how these transactions would appear in the current accounts of the partners and what balances would be shown in the trial balance.

Solution

A – current account

	£		£
Drawings	6,000	Profit for year	10,000
Balance c/d	4,000		
	———		———
	10,000		10,000
	———		———
		Balance b/d	4,000

B – current account

	£		£
Drawings	8,000	Profit for year	10,000
Balance c/d	2,000		
	———		———
	10,000		10,000
	———		———
		Balance b/d	2,000

Trial balance extract

	Dr	Cr
Capital accounts – A		15,000
– B		15,000
Current accounts– A		4,000
– B		2,000

1.6 Columnar accounts

In some partnerships the ledger accounts for capital and current accounts are produced in columnar form which means that each partner has a column in a joint capital and current account.

Example

Using the previous example of A and B we will see how their capital and current accounts would look if the ledger accounts were in columnar form.

Solution

Capital accounts

	A £	B £		A £	B £
			Bank	15,000	15,000

Current accounts

	A £	B £		A £	B £
Drawings	6,000	8,000	Profit for year	10,000	10,000
Balance c/d	4,000	2,000			
	10,000	10,000		10,000	10,000
			Balance b/d	4,000	2,000

Remember that the capital account is only used for recording the capital paid into the business by each partner. The profit earned and the drawings made by each partner are recorded in the current accounts.

 Activity 1

Continuing with the partnership of A and B, in the year 20X2 A paid a further £5,000 of capital into the business.

The profit of the business for the year was £28,000 and this is to be shared equally between A and B.

During the year A had cash drawings of £12,000 and B had cash drawings of £13,000.

Record these transactions in the capital and current accounts of A and B and show the balances on these accounts that would appear in the trial balance at the end of 20X2.

Capital account – A

	£		£
		Balance b/d	15,000
	———		———
	———		———

Capital account – B

	£		£
		Balance b/d	15,000
	———		———
	———		———

Current account – A

	£		£
		Balance b/d	4,000
	———		———
	———		———

Current account – B

	£		£
		Balance b/d	2,000
	———		———
	———		———

Trial balance extract

	Dr £	Cr £
Capital account – A		
Capital account – B		
Current account – A		
Current account – B		

1.7 Debit balances on current accounts

In some instances a partner may withdraw more in cash drawings than is owing to him out of accumulated profits. In this case the partner's current account will show a debit balance.

 Example

Suppose that the balance on a partner's current account at the start of the year is a credit balance of £3,000.

His share of profit for the year is £17,000 and he has £22,000 of drawings.

Show the partner's current account for the year.

Solution

Current account

	£		£
Drawings	22,000	Balance b/d	3,000
		Profit share	17,000
		Balance c/d	2,000
	———		———
	22,000		22,000
	———		———
Balance b/d	2,000		

The balance on the current account is a debit balance and would be shown in the trial balance as such.

Always assume that any balances given for partners' current accounts are credit balances unless you are specifically told otherwise.

2 Appropriation of profit

2.1 Appropriation account

We have already seen how the profit of a partnership business is split between the partners in the business according to their profit sharing ratio and is credited to their current accounts.

The actual splitting up of the profit is done in a profit appropriation account. This can either take the form of another ledger account or it can be shown vertically.

2.2 Salaries

In some partnership agreements it is specified that one or more partners will receive a salary to reflect their level of work in the partnership. This is part of the appropriation of profit and must take place before the profit share.

2.3 Interest on capital

As partners will often have contributed different amounts of capital into the partnership, again the partnership agreement may specify that a rate of interest is allowed to each partner on their outstanding balances. This is part of the appropriation of the profit for the period and must take place before the final profit share.

2.4 Drawings

Drawings do not go through the appropriation account, they are instead debited to the current accounts but during the year they will be recorded in a drawings account for each partner and then transferred to the current account at the year end. This represents a reduction in the partner's capital.

2.5 Interest on drawings

To penalise those partners who take out drawings from the business, the partnership may charge interest on drawings. Interest may be charged on all drawings or only those above a certain level. This results in a reduction in the amount of profit that the partner is allocated.

A proforma appropriation account is shown below for a partnership with two partners A and B for the year-ended 31 Dec 20X7. Note this is to illustrate the layout of the account and the figures have been included purely for the purposes of the illustration.

	Year ended 31 Dec 20X7 £	Total £
Net profit		100,000
Salaries		
A	–	
B	(15,000)	(15,000)
	————	
Interest on capital		
A	(5,000)	
B	(7,000)	(12,000)
	————	
Interest on drawings		
A	5,000	
B	–	5,000
	————	
Profit available for distribution		78,000
Profit share		
A	(39,000)	
B	(39,000)	(78,000)
	————	————
Balance		Nil
		————

Note

1   There are four categories of appropriations that can be entered into the appropriation account

(a)   Salaries

(b)   Interest on capital

(c)   Interest on drawings

(d)   Profit share

2   If any of the categories change during the year then it is easier to have two columns for the periods when the change takes place which are then combined in the total column. The column headings might look as follows.

	1 Jan 20X7 to 30 Sept 20X7	1 Oct 20X7 to 31 Dec 20X7	Total

We shall study an example of this later in the chapter.

Example

X, Y and Z are in partnership sharing profits in the ratio 3:2:1

The profits for the year to 30 June 20X7 were £100,000.

Z receives a salary of £12,000 per annum.

The partners' capital accounts have balance b/d of £50,000, £30,000 and £10,000 respectively. Interest for the year is calculated as 5% of the capital balance b/d.

Produce the appropriation account for the year.

Solution

	Year ended 30 June 20X7 £	Total £
Net profit		100,000
Salaries:		
X		
Y		
Z	(12,000)	(12,000)
Interest on capital		
X (50,000 × 5%)	(2,500)	
Y (30,000 × 5%)	(1,500)	
Z (10,000 × 5%)	(500)	(4,500)
Profit available for distribution		83,500
Profit share		
X (83,500 × 3/6)	(41,750)	
Y (83,500 × 2/6)	(27,833)	
Z (83,500 × 1/6)	(13,917)	(83,500)
Balance		Nil

Example

A and B are in partnership sharing profits equally and, for the year 20X1, the partnership made a profit of £20,000.

We will show how the partnership profit is appropriated in both a ledger appropriation account and a vertical appropriation account.

Solution

Ledger appropriation account

The net profit of the partnership is shown as a credit balance, amount owing to the partners, in the appropriation account.

Appropriation account

	£		£
		Balance b/d	20,000

A journal entry will then be put through for the split of the profit.

Debit Appropriation account – A's profit   £10,000
Debit Appropriation account – B's profit   £10,000

Credit A's current account   £10,000
Credit B's current account   £10,000

The appropriation account and the current accounts can then be written up:

Appropriation account

	£		£
Current account – A	10,000	Balance b/d	20,000
Current account – B	10,000		
	20,000		20,000

Current accounts

	A £	B £		A £	B £
			Appropriation account	£10,000	£10,000

Vertical appropriation account

	£
Net profit for the year	20,000
Profit share – A	10,000
Profit share – B	10,000
	20,000

Example

C and D are in partnership and their capital balances are £100,000 and £60,000 respectively.

During 20X4 the profit made by the partnership totalled £80,000.

The partnership agreement specifies the following:

- D receives a salary of £15,000 per annum.
- Both partners receive interest on their capital balances at the rate of 5%.
- The profit sharing ratio is 2:1.

We will now appropriate the profit and write up the partners' current accounts.

C made £37,000 of drawings during the year and D made £33,500 of drawings during the year.

The balance b/ds on their current accounts were both £1,000 credit balances.

Solution

The salary and the interest on capital must be deducted first from the available profits.

The remainder is then split in the profit share ratio of 2:1.

This means that C gets two thirds of the remaining profit whilst D gets one third of the remaining profit.

Appropriation account

		£	£
Profit for the year			80,000
Salary	– D	15,000	
Interest on capital	– C (100,000 × 5%)	5,000	
	D (60,000 × 5%)	3,000	
		———	(23,000)
			———
Profit available for profit share			57,000
			———
Profit share	– C (57,000 × 2/3)		38,000
	D (57,000 × 1/3)		19,000
			———
			57,000
			———

The current accounts can now be written up to reflect the profit share and the drawings for the year.

Current account

	C £	D £		C £	D £
Drawings	37,000	33,500	Balance b/d	1,000	1,000
			Salary		15,000
			Interest on capital	5,000	3,000
Balance c/d	7,000	4,500	Profit share	38,000	19,000
	44,000	38,000		44,000	38,000
			Balance b/d	7,000	4,500

 Example

Hamish and Campbell started a business on 1 January 20X6, investing £20,000 and £14,000 respectively.

In the first year of trade, the business made £25,000 profit.

They have set up the following partnership agreement:

- Neither partner receives a salary.

- Interest on capital is to be provided at 4%.

- Interest on drawings is to be charged at 2%.

- The balance of profit is to be split in the ratio 3:2.

Both Hamish and Campbell withdrew £5,000 from the business on 1 July 20X6.

Show how this information appears in the partners' capital and current accounts and in the statement of financial position.

Solution

	Year ended 31 Dec X6 £	Total £
Net profit		25,000
Interest on capital		
Hamish	(800)	
Campbell	(560)	(1,360)
Interest on drawings (W)		
Hamish	50	
Campbell	50	100
Profit available for distribution		23,740
Profit share		
Hamish	(14,244)	
Campbell	(9,496)	(23,740)
Balance		Nil

Working – interest on drawings £5,000 × 2% × 6/12 = 50

Hamish total: £800 – £50 + £14,244 = £14,994

Campbell total: £560 - £50 + £9,496 = £10,006

Capital account

	Hamish £	Campbell £		Hamish £	Campbell £
Bal c/d	20,000	14,000	01.01.X6	20,000	14,000
	20,000	14,000		20,000	14,000
			Bal b/d	20,000	14,000

Current account

	Hamish £	Campbell £		Hamish £	Campbell £
Drawings	5,000	5,000	Profit share	14,994	10,006
Bal c/d	9,994	5,006			
	14,994	10,006		14,994	10,006
			Bal b/d	9,994	5,006

Statement of financial position extract:

		£	£
Capital accounts:	Hamish	20,000	
	Campbell	14,000	
			34,000
Current accounts:	Hamish	9,994	
	Campbell	5,006	
			15,000
			49,000

Activity 2

Nick and Ted are in partnership sharing profits in the ratio of 3:2. During the year ended 30 June 20X4 the partnership made a profit of £120,000.

The partnership agreement states that Ted is to receive a salary of £20,000 and that interest on capital balances is paid at 6% per annum.

The balances on the current accounts, capital accounts and drawings accounts at the year end before the appropriation of profit were as follows:

		£
Capital	– Nick	150,000
	Ted	100,000
Current	– Nick	3,000 (credit)
	Ted	1,000 (debit)
Drawings	– Nick	56,000
	Ted	59,000

Complete the appropriation account and the partners' current accounts after appropriation of profit and transfer of drawings at 30 June 20X4.

Appropriation account

		£	£
Net profit			
Salary	– Ted		
Interest on capital	– Nick		
	Ted		
		———	
			———
Profit available			
			———
Profit share	– Nick		
	Ted		
			———
			———

Current accounts

	Nick £	Ted £		Nick £	Ted £
Balance b/d			Balance b/d		
Drawings			Salary		
			Interest on capital		
Balance c/d			Profit share		
	———	———		———	———
	———	———		———	———
			Balance b/d		

2.6 Partnership losses

Any salaries and interest on capital must be appropriated first to the partners even if the partnership makes a loss or if this appropriation turns a profit into a loss.

Then the loss itself is split between the partners in the profit share ratio by debiting their current accounts. The partners suffer the loss in the same proportion they share the profits.

Example

The partnership of E and F made a profit of £10,000 for the year ended 31 March 20X5.

The partnership agreement states that each partner receives interest on their capital balances of 10% per annum and that E receives a salary of £8,000.

Any remaining profits or losses are split in the ratio of 3:1.

The balances on their capital accounts were £50,000 and £40,000 respectively and neither partner had a balance b/d on their current accounts.

Neither partner made any drawings during the year.

Write up the partnership profit appropriation account and the partners' current accounts for the year.

Appropriation account

		£	£
Partnership profit			10,000
Salary	– E	8,000	
Interest	– E	5,000	
	F	4,000	
		———	(17,000)
			———
Loss to be shared			(7,000)
			———
Loss share	– E (7,000 × 3/4)		(5,250)
	F (7,000 × 1/4)		(1,750)
			———
			(7,000)
			———

Current account

	E £	F £		E £	F £
Loss share	5,250	1,750	Salary	8,000	
Balance c/d	7,750	2,250	Interest	5,000	4,000
	———	———		———	———
	13,000	4,000		13,000	4,000
	———	———		———	———
			Balance b/d	7,750	2,250

Example

A and B each have current account balances of £10,000.

During 20X1 A had drawings of £6,000 and B had drawings of £8,000.

Show how these are entered in the ledger accounts.

Solution

At the year end the drawings accumulated in the drawings accounts are transferred by a journal entry to the current accounts of the partners as follows:

Debit Current account – A   £6,000
Debit Current account – B   £8,000

Credit Drawings account – A   £6,000
Credit Drawings account – B   £8,000

	Drawings account – A			
	£			£
Cash	6,000	Current account		6,000

	Drawings account – B			
	£			£
Cash	8,000	Current account		8,000

	Current accounts				
	A	B		A	B
	£	£		£	£
Drawings	6,000	8,000	Balance b/d	10,000	10,000

3   Changes in the partnership agreement

3.1   Changes in profit share

In some partnerships the partners will decide to change the partnership agreement and the profit share ratio part of the way through the year. In these cases the appropriation of profit must take place in two separate calculations.

Firstly, the profit for the period under the old profit share agreement must be appropriated using the old profit share ratio.

Secondly, the profit for the period after the change must be appropriated using the new profit share ratio.

Unless otherwise stated, it must be assumed that profits accrue evenly throughout the year (i.e. divide the total profit/loss for the year by 12 to work out a monthly profit/loss).

 Example

Bill and Ben are in partnership and the profits of the partnership for the year ended 31 December 20X3 were £60,000.

The partnership agreement at the start of the year was that profits were to be shared equally.

However, on 31 March 20X3 it was decided to change the partnership agreement so that Ben received a salary of £8,000 per annum and the remaining profits were shared in the ratio of 2:1.

Both partners had a balance b/d on their current accounts of £2,000 (credit) and the profits for the year accrued evenly.

Show the appropriation of the profits to the partners' current accounts for the year.

Solution

Step 1

Determine the profit for the first three months of the year and appropriate that according to the old profit share ratio.

	£
Profit (£60,000 × 3/12)	15,000
	————
Bill (15,000 × 1/2)	7,500
Ben (15,000 × 1/2)	7,500
	————
	15,000
	————

Step 2

Determine the profit for the final nine months of the year and appropriate that according to the new profit share ratio.

Profit (£60,000 × 9/12)	45,000
Salary – Ben (£8,000 × 9/12)	(6,000)
	———
Profit to be appropriated	39,000
	———
Profit share – Bill (£39,000 × 2/3)	26,000
Ben (£39,000 × 1/3)	13,000
	———
	39,000
	———

 Example

Consider the previous example and write up the appropriation account for the same information in a columnar form

Solution

	1 Jan – 31 Mar 20X3	1 Apr – 31 Dec 20X3	Total (£)
Profit	**15,000**	**45,000**	**60,000**
Salary			
Ben (£8,000 × 9/12)		6,000	6,000
Profit available for distribution	**15,000**	**39,000**	**54,000**
Profit share			
Bill	7,500	26,000	33,500
Ben	7,500	13,000	20,500
Balance	**Nil**	**Nil**	**Nil**

3.2 Changes in interest

The partnership agreement may be changed during a period so that for example a different rate of interest is paid on capital from a given date in the year.

The profit must be divided into the two periods and interest must be calculated both before and after that date.

Example

A, B and C are in partnership for the year ended 31 December 20X8, sharing profits in the ratio 3:2:1. The net profit for the year was £90,000.

At 1 January 20X8 the partners' capital was

	£
A	50,000
B	30,000
C	20,000

For the period to 30 April 20X8, the partners received interest at 3% on their capital at the beginning of the year. For the remainder of the year they received interest at 4% on their capital at the beginning of the year. Profits accrued evenly throughout the year.

Task 1

Complete the table showing the interest received by the partners during the year for the two separate periods and in total

	1 Jan X8 – 30 Apr X8 £	*1 May X8 – 31 Dec X8* £	*Total* £

Task 2

Prepare the appropriation account for the year to 31 December 20X8.

Solution

Task 1

	1 Jan X8 – 30 Apr X8 £	*1 May X8 – 31 Dec X8* £	*Total* £
Interest			
A	50,000 × 3% × 4/12 = 500	50,000 × 4% × 8/12 = 1,333	1,833
B	30,000 × 3% × 4/12 = 300	30,000 × 4% × 8/12 = 800	1,100
C	20,000 × 3% × 4/12 = 200	20,000 × 4% × 8/12 = 533	733

Task 2

Appropriation account for the year to 31 December 20X8

	1 Jan X8 – 30 Apr X8 £	1 May X8 – 31 Dec X8 £	Total £
Net profit	**30,000**	**60,000**	**90,000**
A	500	1,333	1,833
B	300	800	1,100
C	200	533	733
Profit available for distribution	**29,000**	**57,334**	**86,334**
Profit share			
A	29,000 × 3/6 = 14,500	57,334 × 3/6 = 28,667	43,167
B	29,000 × 2/6 = 9,667	57,334 × 2/6 = 19,111	28,778
C	29,000 × 1/6 = 4,833	57,334 × 1/6 = 9,556	14,389
Balance	**Nil**	**Nil**	**Nil**

 Activity 3

During the year ended 30 June 20X4, the partnership of Jill, Jane and Jan made a profit of £100,000.

Up until 31 March 20X4 the profit share ratio was 2:2:1

However, the partnership agreement was changed on 31 March 20X4 so that Jane was to receive a salary of £16,000 per annum and that the profits were to be shared equally.

The balances on the partners' current accounts and drawings accounts at 30 June 20X4 were as follows:

			£
Current accounts	–	Jill	3,000
		Jane	2,000
		Jan	1,000
Drawings accounts	–	Jill	38,000
		Jane	40,000
		Jan	25,000

Prepare the appropriation account and the partners' current accounts for the year. Assume that profits accrued evenly throughout the year.

Appropriation account

	£
Profit to 31 March 20X4	_____
Profit share – Jill	
Jane	
Jan	
	_____
	_____
Profit to 30 June 20X4	
Salary Jane	
	_____
Profit available	
	_____
Profit share – Jill	
Jane	
Jan	
	_____
	_____

Current accounts

	Jill £	Jane £	Jan £		Jill £	Jane £	Jan £
Drawings				Balance b/d			
				Profit share			
				Salary			
Balance c/d				Profit share			
				Balance c/d			
	____	____	____		____	____	____
	____	____	____		____	____	____
Balance b/d				Balance b/d			

3.3   Changes in salary, interest and profit share

The partnership agreement may be changed during a period so that all three variables (salary, interest and profit share) are altered during the period.

The profit must be divided into the two periods (assuming that all the changes are effective from the same day in the period) and any changes put into the appropriate period.

Example

X, Y and Z are in partnership for the year ended 31 December 20X8.

At the start of the year they share profits in the ratio 2:2:1. The net profit for the year was £144,000.

At 1 January 20X8 the partners' capital was

	£
X	100,000
Y	50,000
Z	40,000

For the period to 31 May 20X8, the partners received interest at 3% on their capital at the beginning of the year.

For the remainder of the year they received interest at 4% on their capital at the beginning of the year.

For the period to 31 May 20X8 Z received a salary of £18,000 per annum. For the remainder of the year Z received no salary and the profit share was changed to 3:2:2.

During the year the partners each drew £2,000 per month in drawings.

Task 1

Complete the table showing the interest received by the partners during the year for the two separate periods and in total.

	1 Jan 0X – 31 May X8 £	1 June X8 – 31 Dec X8 £	Total £

Task 2

Complete the table showing the appropriation account for the partnership for both periods down to the line for the 'profits available for distribution'.

	1 Jan X8 – 31 May X8 £	1 June X8 – 31 Dec X8 £	Total £
Net profit			
Salaries			
X			
Y			
Z			
Interest			
X			
Y			
Z			
Profits available for distribution			

Task 3

Complete the appropriation account showing the profit shares for the partners and the balance left for distribution if any.

Task 4

Explain how drawings are entered in the books of accounts.

Solution

Task 1

	1 Jan X8 – 31 May X8 £	1 June X8 – 31 Dec X8 £	Total £
Interest			
X	100,000 × 3% × 5/12 = 1,250	100,000 × 4% × 7/12 = 2,333	3,583
Y	50,000 × 3% × 5/12 = 625	50,000 × 4% × 7/12 = 1,167	1,792
Z	40,000 × 3% × 5/12 = 500	40,000 × 4% × 7/12 = 933	1,433

Task 2 and 3

Appropriation account for the year to 31 December 2008

	1 Jan X8 – 31 May X8 £	1 June X8 – 31 Dec X8 £	Total £
Net profit	**60,000**	**84,000**	**144,000**
Salaries			
X			
Y			
Z (18,000 × 5/12)	7,500		7,500
Interest			
X	1,250	2,333	3,583
Y	625	1,167	1,792
Z	500	933	1,433
Profit available for distribution	**50,125**	**79,567**	**129,692**
Profit share			
X	(50,125 × 2/5) 20,050	(79,567 × 3/7) 34,100	54,150
Y	(50,125 × 2/5) 20,050	(79,567 × 2/7) 22,733	42,783
Z	(50,125 × 1/5) 10,025	(79,567 × 2/7) 22,734	32,759
Balance	**Nil**	**Nil**	**Nil**

Task 4

Drawings are not an expense of the business or a form of remuneration for the partners.

They are simply the partners taking money out of the business on account of the profit share that they will eventually receive.

The drawings are therefore not entered in the partnership statement of profit or loss, but are entered as a debit in the partners' current accounts.

4 Admission of a new partner

4.1 Introduction

When a new partner is admitted to the partnership then the partners will agree a certain sum of cash that the new partner must pay for his share in the partnership. The basic double entry for the cash that the new partner brings into the partnership is:

Debit Bank account

Credit New partner's capital account

However, there is a complication in that we need to consider the goodwill of the partnership.

4.2 Goodwill

As well as the net assets that a partnership have recorded in their ledger accounts such as machinery, motor vehicles, receivables, inventory, payables, etc, most businesses will have another asset which is not recorded in the ledger accounts, being goodwill.

Goodwill comes about due to the excellence or reputation of the business. It can be due to good quality products, good after sales service, good location, excellence of employees and many other factors.

The problem with goodwill is that not only is it very difficult to measure in monetary terms but it is also very volatile.

Goodwill is essentially the value of the business as a whole over and above the value of the recorded net assets. Unless the business is actually being sold then this total value is only an estimate.

A further problem is the nature of goodwill. Suppose that the goodwill of a restaurant business has been built up due to the reputation of the head chef; if that chef leaves or there is a bout of food poisoning in the restaurant, the goodwill is wiped out immediately.

Due to these problems, such goodwill is not recognised in the financial statements of a business. However, there is little doubt that it does exist in many businesses.

4.3 Goodwill and admission of a new partner

When a new partner is admitted to a partnership he will be buying not only a share of the recorded net assets of the business but also a share of the unrecorded goodwill in the business.

This must be recognised in the accounting procedures.

Step 1

Immediately before the admission of the new partner, the amount of goodwill that the old partners have built up must be recognised and shared out between the partners. This is done by the following double entry:

Debit   Goodwill account with the estimated value of the goodwill

Credit Old partners' capital accounts in the old profit share ratio

Step 2

The new partner will now be admitted and the cash that he brings into the partnership is accounted for by:

Debit   Bank account

Credit New partner's capital account

Step 3

Finally the goodwill must be eliminated from the books. This is done by:

Debit   New partners' capital accounts in the new profit share ratio

Credit Goodwill account with the value of the goodwill

By this stage the goodwill has been taken out of the accounts again and the partners' capital account balances have been adjusted to account for the old partners' share of the goodwill they have earned and the new partner's purchase of not only a share of the recorded net assets but also his share of the unrecorded asset goodwill.

 Example

Pete and Paul have been in partnership for a number of years sharing profits equally.

The balance on Pete's capital account is £100,000 and the balance on Paul's capital account is £80,000.

They have decided to admit a new partner to the partnership, Phil. Phil will contribute £60,000 in cash to the partnership on his admission and the profit share ratio after he is admitted will be two fifths of profits for Pete and Paul and one fifth of profits for Phil.

The goodwill in the partnership is estimated to be £30,000.

Write up the partners' capital accounts to reflect the admission of Phil.

Solution

Step 1

Set up the (temporary) goodwill account and credit the old partners in the old profit share ratio in their capital accounts.

Goodwill account

	£		£
Capital accounts	30,000		

Capital accounts

	Pete £	Paul £			Pete £	Paul £
				Balance b/d	100,000	80,000
				Goodwill	15,000	15,000

Step 2

Introduce the new partner and his capital

Capital accounts

	Pete £	Paul £	Phil £		Pete £	Paul £	Phil £
				Bal b/d	100,000	80,000	
				Goodwill	15,000	15,000	
				Bank			60,000

(NB: the bank T account is not shown).

Step 3

Eliminate the goodwill by debiting all of the partners' capital accounts in the new profit share ratio and crediting the goodwill account.

Goodwill account

	£		£
Capital accounts	30,000	Capital accounts	30,000

Capital accounts

	Pete £	Paul £	Phil £		Pete £	Paul £	Phil £
Goodwill	12,000	12,000	6,000	Bal b/d	100,000	80,000	
				Goodwill	15,000	15,000	
Bal c/d	103,000	83,000	54,000	Bank			60,000
	115,000	95,000	60,000		115,000	95,000	60,000
				Bal b/d	103,000	83,000	54,000

What has happened here is that with his £60,000 Phil has purchased a share of the recorded net assets of the business worth £54,000 and £6,000 of goodwill, as shown by his capital account.

He has effectively purchased this from Pete and Paul for £3,000 each as their capital balances have increased by £3,000 in total each.

Activity 4

Karl and Len have been in partnership for a number of years sharing profits in the ratio of 2:1.

They have capital account balances of £80,000 and £50,000 respectively.

On 30 June 20X4 they have invited Nina to join the partnership and she is to introduce £35,000 of capital.

From this date the profits are to be shared with two fifths to Karl and Len and one fifth to Nina. The goodwill of the partnership at 30 June 20X4 is estimated to be £15,000.

Write up the partners' capital accounts to reflect the admission of Nina.

Capital accounts

Karl £	Len £	Nina £		Karl £	Len £	Nina £
___	___	___		___	___	___
___	___	___		___	___	___

5 Retirement of a partner

5.1 Introduction

When a partner retires from a partnership the full amounts that are due to him must be calculated. This will include his capital account balance, his current account balance plus his share of any goodwill that the partnership has at the retirement date. The adjustments in the partners' capital accounts to reflect all of this are very similar to those for the admission of a new partner.

5.2 Accounting adjustments

On the retirement of a partner there are a number of accounting adjustments that must take place to ensure that the full amounts due to the retiring partner are paid to him.

Step 1

Transfer the retiring partner's current account balance to his capital account so that we are only dealing with one account.

Debit   **Partners' current account balance**

Credit **Partners' capital account**

Step 2

Recognise the goodwill that has been built up in the partnership by temporarily setting up a goodwill account and crediting all of the partners with their share of the goodwill.

Debit   **Goodwill account with the value of the goodwill on the retirement date**

Credit **Partners' capital accounts in their profit sharing ratio**

Step 3

Now the retiring partner has the total balance that is due to him in his capital account. He must then be paid off. The simplest method is to pay him what is due to him in cash:

Debit   **Retiring partner's capital account with the balance due**

Credit **Bank account**

The partnership may not have enough cash to pay off all that is due to the partner so, instead, the retiring partner leaves some or all of what is due to him as a loan to the partnership that will be repaid in the future.

Debit   **Retiring partner's capital account**

Credit **Loan account**

Step 4

We must now remove the goodwill from the ledger by:

Debit   **Remaining partners' capital accounts in profit share ratio**

Credit **Goodwill account with the value of the goodwill**

Example

Rob, Marc and Di have been in partnership for a number of years sharing profits in the ratio of 3:2:1.

On 1 March 20X3 Rob retired from the partnership and at that date the goodwill was valued at £60,000.

The other two partners agreed with Rob that he would be paid £20,000 of what was due to him in cash and the remainder would be a loan to the partnership.

After Rob's retirement Marc and Di are to share profits in the ratio of 2:1.

The capital account and current account balances at 1 March 20X3 were as follows:

		£
Capital accounts	– Rob	65,000
	Marc	55,000
	Di	40,000
Current accounts	– Rob	8,000
	Marc	5,000
	Di	2,000

Write up the partners' capital accounts to reflect the retirement of Rob.

Solution

Step 1

Transfer Rob's current account balance to his capital account.

Capital accounts

	Rob £	Marc £	Di £		Rob £	Marc £	Di £
				Bal b/d	65,000	55,000	40,000
				Current a/c	8,000		

Current accounts

	Rob £	Marc £	Di £		Rob £	Marc £	Di £
Capital a/c	8,000			Bal b/d	8,000	5,000	2,000

Step 2

Temporarily open up a goodwill account and credit the partners' capital accounts in the old profit sharing ratio.

Goodwill account

	£		£
Capital accounts	60,000		

Capital accounts

	Rob £	Marc £	Di £		Rob £	Marc £	Di £
				Bal b/d	65,000	55,000	40,000
				Current a/c	8,000		
				Goodwill	30,000	20,000	10,000

Step 3

Pay Rob off as agreed – £20,000 in cash and the remainder as a loan.

Capital accounts

	Rob £	Marc £	Di £		Rob £	Marc £	Di £
Bank	20,000			Bal b/d	65,000	55,000	40,000
Loan	83,000			Current a/c	8,000		
				Goodwill	30,000	20,000	10,000
	103,000				103,000		

Step 4

Remove the goodwill from the ledger with a credit to the goodwill account and a debit to the remaining partners' capital accounts in the new profit share ratio.

Goodwill account

	£		£
Capital accounts	60,000	Capital accounts	60,000

Capital accounts

	Rob £	Marc £	Di £		Rob £	Marc £	Di £
Bank	20,000			Bal b/d	65,000	55,000	40,000
Loan	83,000			Current a/c	8,000		
Goodwill		40,000	20,000				
Bal c/d	–	35,000	30,000	Goodwill	30,000	20,000	10,000
	103,000	75,000	50,000		103,000	75,000	50,000
				Bal b/d		35,000	30,000

You can see that Marc's capital account balance has reduced by £20,000 and that Di's has reduced by £10,000.

They have effectively been charged with the £30,000 of goodwill that has to be paid to Rob on his retirement. Consequently Marc and Di will have a greater share of profits.

 Activity 5

M, N and P have been in partnership for a number of years sharing profits equally.

On 30 June 20X4 M is to retire from the partnership and thereafter N and P will share profits equally.

The value of the goodwill of the partnership is estimated to be £30,000 and M has agreed to leave the entire amount due to him on loan to the partnership.

The capital and current account balances at 30 June 20X4 are as follows:

Current accounts

	M £	N £	P £		M £	N £	P £
				Balance b/d	4,000	5,000	6,000

Write up the partners' capital accounts to reflect the retirement of M.

Capital accounts

	M £	N £	P £		M £	N £	P £
				Balance b/d	50,000	40,000	30,000
	——	——	——		——	——	——
	——	——	——		——	——	——

6 Preparing financial statements for a partnership

6.1 Statement of profit or loss

The first stage in preparing a partnership's financial statements from either a trial balance or an extended trial balance is to prepare the statement of profit or loss. This will be exactly the same as the preparation of a statement of profit or loss for a sole trader with the same types of adjustments such as depreciation expenses, closing inventory, irrecoverable and doubtful debts and accruals and prepayments

6.2 Appropriation of profit

The next stage is to take the net profit from the statement of profit or loss and prepare an appropriation account in order to split the profit between the partners in the profit share ratio to include in their current accounts.

Remember that if the profit share ratio has changed during the period, the appropriation must be done in two separate calculations.

6.3 Drawings

In the trial balance there will be account balances for each partner's drawings, these must be transferred to the partners' current accounts and the balance on each partner's current account identified.

6.4 Statement of financial position

The final stage is to prepare the statement of financial position of the partnership. The top part of the statement of financial position will be exactly the same as that for a sole trader. Only the capital section of the statement of financial position is different. Here the capital account balances and the current account balances for each partner are listed and totalled, and this total should agree with the net assets total of the top part of the statement of financial position.

 Example

A, B and C are in partnership with a partnership agreement that B receives a salary of £8,000 per annum and C a salary of £12,000 per annum.

Interest on capital is allowed at 4% per annum and the profits are shared in the ratio of 2:1:1.

The list of ledger balances at the year end of 31 March 20X4 are given below:

		£
Drawings	A	43,200
	B	26,000
	C	30,200
Purchases ledger control account		56,000
Bank balance		2,800
Current accounts at 1 April 20X3	A	3,500
	B	7,000
	C	4,200
Purchases		422,800
Inventory at 1 April 20X3		63,000
Capital accounts	A	42,000
	B	32,200
	C	14,000
Sales ledger control account		75,600
Revenue		651,000
Non-current assets at cost		112,000
Accumulated depreciation at 1 April 20X3		58,900
Allowance for doubtful debts at 1 April 20X3		2,000
Expenses		95,200

You are also given the following information:

(i)   Inventory at 31 March 20X4 has been valued at £70,000.

(ii) Depreciation for the year has yet to be provided at 20% on cost.

(iii) An irrecoverable debt of £5,600 is to be written off and an allowance for doubtful debts is to be 2% of the remaining receivables.

(iv) Expenses of £7,000 are to be accrued.

Task 1

Draw up are initial trial balance at 31 March 20X4

Trial balance at 31 March 20X4

		£	£
Drawings	A	43,200	
	B	26,000	
	C	30,200	
Purchases ledger control account			56,000
Bank balance		2,800	
Current accounts at 1 April 20X3	A		3,500
	B		7,000
	C		4,200
Purchases		422,800	
Capital accounts	A		42,000
	B		32,200
	C		14,000
Inventory at 1 April 20X3		63,000	
Sales ledger control account		75,600	
Sales			651,000
Non-current assets at cost		112,000	
Accumulated depreciation at 1 April 20X3			58,900
Allowance for doubtful debts at 1 April 20X3			2,000
Expenses		95,200	
		870,800	870,800

Task 2

Prepare the statement of profit or loss for the year ended 31 March 20X4.

Statement of profit or loss for the year ending 31 March 20X4

		£	£
Revenue			651,000
Less:	Cost of sales		
	Opening inventory	63,000	
	Purchases	422,800	
		———	
		485,800	
Less:	Closing inventory	(70,000)	
		———	415,800
			———
Gross profit			235,200
Less:	Expenses (95,200 + 7,000)	102,200	
	Depreciation (20% × 112,000)	22,400	
	Irrecoverable debts	5,600	
	Allowance in doubtful debt adjustment		
	(2% × (75,600 – 5,600) – 2,000)	(600)	
		———	
Total expenses			129,600
			———
Net profit			105,600
			———

Task 3

Prepare the appropriation account.

Appropriation account

			£	£
Net profit				105,600
Salaries	–	B	8,000	
		C	12,000	
			———	(20,000)
Interest on capital	–	A (42,000 × 4%)	1,680	
		B (32,200 × 4%)	1,288	
		C (14,000 × 4%)	560	
			———	
				(3,528)
				———
Profit for profit share				82,072
A (82,072 × 2/4)			41,036	
B (82,072 × 1/4)			20,518	
C (82,072 × 1/4)			20,518	
			———	
				82,072
				———

Task 4

Prepare the partners current account to include salaries, interest, profit share and drawings.

Current accounts

	A £	B £	C £		A £	B £	C £
Drawings	43,200	26,000	30,200	Balance b/d	3,500	7,000	4,200
				Salaries		8,000	12,000
				Interest on cap	1,680	1,288	560
Balance c/d	3,016	10,806	7,078	Profit share	41,036	20,518	20,518
	———	———	———		———	———	———
	46,216	36,806	37,278		46,216	36,806	37,278
	———	———	———		———	———	———
				Balance b/d	3,016	10,806	7,078

Task 5

Prepare the statement of financial position for the partnership at 31 March 20X4

Statement of financial position as at 31 March 20X4

	£	£	£
Non-current assets at cost			112,000
Accumulated depreciation (58,900 + 22,400)			(81,300)
			————
Carrying value			30,700
Current assets			
Inventory		70,000	
Trade receivables	70,000		
Less: Allowance for doubtful debts	(1,400)		
	————	68,600	
Bank		2,800	
		————	
		141,400	
Current liabilities:			
Trade payables	56,000		
Accruals	7,000		
	————		
		(63,000)	
		————	
Net current assets			78,400
			————
Net assets			109,100
			————

		£	£
Capital accounts	A	42,000	
	B	32,200	
	C	14,000	
		————	
			88,200
Current accounts	A	3,016	
	B	10,806	
	C	7,078	
		————	
			20,900
			————
			109,100
			————

Activity 6

The partnership of Lyle and Tate has made a net profit of £58,000 for the year ended 30 June 20X3.

The partnership agreement is that Tate receives a salary of £8,000 per annum and that the profits are split in the ratio of 3:2.

The list of statement of financial position balances at 30 June 20X3 are given below:

			£
Capital accounts	–	Lyle	75,000
		Tate	50,000
Current accounts at 1 July 20X2	–	Lyle	3,000
		Tate	2,000
Drawings	–	Lyle	28,000
		Tate	24,000
Non-current assets at cost			100,000
Accumulated depreciation at 30 June 20X3			30,000
Inventory at 30 June 20X3			44,000
Trade receivables			38,000
Bank			10,000
Trade payables			26,000

Prepare the appropriation account

Appropriation account

	£	£
Net profit		
Salary – Tate		
	———	
Profit available		
	———	
Profit share – Lyle		
Tate		
	———	
	———	

Write up and balance the partners' current accounts.

Current accounts

	Lyle £	Tate £		Lyle £	Tate £
Drawings			Balance b/d		
Balance c/d			Appropriation a/c		
	——	——		——	——
	——	——		——	——
			Balance b/d		

Prepare the statement of financial position as at 30 June 20X3.

Statement of financial position as at 30 June 20X3

	£	£
Non-current assets at cost		
Accumulated depreciation		
		——
Current assets		
Inventory		
Trade Receivables		
Bank		
	——	
Less: Trade payables		
Net current assets		
		——
Net assets		
		——
Capital accounts	Lyle	
	Tate	
		——
Current accounts	Lyle	
	Tate	
	——	
		——
		——

Partnership accounts will always appear in the AAT exam but you will never have to deal with a partnership with more than three partners.

Activity 7

1   What is the double entry when a partner withdraws goods from the partnership?

Debit

Credit

2   What is the double entry required to transfer a partner's drawings from the drawings account to the current account? (complete the account name in the box)

Debit

Credit

3   What is the double entry for interest on a partner's capital?

Debit

Credit

4   What is the goodwill of a partnership?

_____

_____

_____

_____

5   Is goodwill normally recorded as a permanent asset of a partnership?

No   ☐

Yes   ☐

7 Summary

In this chapter we have dealt with all aspects of partnership accounts which are required for the exam. The AAT examination will always feature partnership accounting so this is an important area. In terms of preparing financial statements for a partnership, the preparation of the statement of profit or loss is exactly the same as that for a sole trader; therefore in this chapter we have concentrated on the areas of difference between a sole trader and a partnership.

When partners pay capital into the partnership this is recorded in the partner's individual capital account. The profit of the partnership must then be shared between the partners according to the partnership agreement. This may include salaries for some partners, interest on capital as well as the final profit share ratio. All aspects of sharing out the profit take place in the appropriation account which can take the form of a ledger account or a vertical statement. The appropriated profit is credited to the partners' current accounts and their current accounts are debited with their drawings for the period. The balances on the partners' capital accounts and current accounts are listed in the bottom part of the statement of financial position and should be equal in total to the net assets total of the top part of the statement of financial position.

You may also be required to deal with changes in the partnership. The most straightforward of these is a change in the profit share ratio during the period. This requires a separate appropriation for the period before the change according to the old profit share ratio and then for the period after the change using the new profit share ratio.

If a partner is admitted to the partnership or a partner retires then the goodwill of the partnership has to be considered. The goodwill is not recorded in the partnership books but upon a change, such as an admission or retirement, it must be brought into account to ensure that each partner is given full credit, not only for the recorded assets but also for the goodwill. The treatment is fundamentally the same for both an admission and a retirement. The goodwill account is temporarily set up as a debit (an asset) and the partners' capital accounts are credited in the old profit share ratio. The goodwill is then removed with a credit entry to the goodwill account and debits to the partners' capital accounts in the new profit share ratio.

Answers to chapter activities

Activity 1

Capital account – A

	£		£
Balance c/d	20,000	Balance b/d	15,000
		Bank	5,000
	20,000		20,000
		Balance b/d	20,000

Capital account – B

	£		£
Balance c/d	15,000	Balance b/d	15,000
	15,000		15,000
		Balance b/d	15,000

Current account – A

	£		£
Drawings	12,000	Balance b/d	4,000
Balance c/d	6,000	Profit	14,000
	18,000		18,000
		Balance b/d	6,000

Current account – B

	£		£
Drawings	13,000	Balance b/d	2,000
Balance c/d	3,000	Profit	14,000
	16,000		16,000
		Balance b/d	3,000

Trial balance extract

	Dr £	Cr £
Capital account – A		20,000
Capital account – B		15,000
Current account – A		6,000
Current account – B		3,000

Activity 2

Appropriation account

		£	£
Net profit			120,000
Salary – Ted		20,000	
Interest on capital –	Nick (6% × 150,000)	9,000	
	Ted (6% × 100,000)	6,000	
			(35,000)
Profit available			85,000
Profit share –	Nick (85,000 × 3/5)		51,000
	Ted (85,000 × 2/5)		34,000
			85,000

Current accounts

	Nick £	Ted £		Nick £	Ted £
Balance b/d		1,000	Balance b/d	3,000	
Drawings	56,000	59,000	Salary		20,000
			Interest on capital	9,000	6,000
Balance c/d	7,000		Profit share	51,000	34,000
	63,000	60,000		63,000	60,000
			Balance b/d		7,000

Activity 3

Appropriation account

1.7.X3 to 31.3.X4

		£
Profit to 31 March 20X4 (100,000 × 9/12)		75,000

Profit share	–	Jill (75,000 × 2/5)	30,000
		Jane (75,000 × 2/5)	30,000
		Jan (75,000 × 1/5)	15,000
			75,000

1.4.X4 – 30.6.X4

		£
Profit to 30 June 20X4 (100,000 x 3/12)		25,000
Salary	Jane (16,000 × 3/12)	(4,000)
Profit available		21,000

Profit share	–	Jill (21,000 × 1/3)	7,000
		Jane (21,000 x 1/3)	7,000
		Jan (21,000 x 1/3)	7,000
			21,000

Current accounts

	Jill £	Jane £	Jan £		Jill £	Jane £	Jan £
Drawings	38,000	40,000	25,000	Balance b/d	3,000	2,000	1,000
				Profit share	30,000	30,000	15,000
				Salary		4,000	
Balance c/d	2,000	3,000		Profit share	7,000	7,000	7,000
				Balance c/d			2,000
	40,000	43,000	25,000		40,000	43,000	25,000
Balance b/d			2,000	Balance b/d	2,000	3,000	

Activity 4

Capital accounts

	Karl £	Len £	Nina £		Karl £	Len £	Nina £
				Balance b/d	80,000	50,000	
Goodwill	6,000	6,000	3,000	Goodwill	10,000	5,000	
Balance c/d	84,000	49,000	32,000	Bank			35,000
	90,000	55,000	35,000		90,000	55,000	35,000
				Balance b/d	84,000	49,000	32,000

Activity 5

Capital accounts

	M £	N £	P £		M £	N £	P £
Goodwill		15,000	15,000	Balance b/d	50,000	40,000	30,000
Loan	64,000			Current a/c	4,000		
Balance c/d		35,000	25,000	Goodwill	10,000	10,000	10,000
	64,000	50,000	40,000		64,000	50,000	40,000
				Balance b/d		35,000	25,000

Activity 6

Appropriation account

	£	£
Net profit		58,000
Salary – Tate		(8,000)
Profit available		50,000
Profit share – Lyle (50,000 × 3/5)	30,000	
Tate (50,000 × 2/5)	20,000	
		50,000

Current accounts

	Lyle £	Tate £		Lyle £	Tate £
Drawings	28,000	24,000	Balance b/d	3,000	2,000
Balance c/d	5,000	6,000	Appropriation a/c	30,000	28,000
	33,000	30,000		33,000	30,000
			Balance b/d	5,000	6,000

Statement of financial position as at 30 June 20X3

	£	£
Non-current assets at cost		100,000
Accumulated depreciation		(30,000)
		70,000
Current assets:		
Inventory	44,000	
Trade receivables	38,000	
Bank	10,000	
	92,000	
Less: Trade payables	(26,000)	
Net current assets		66,000
Net assets		136,000
Capital accounts – Lyle		75,000
Tate		50,000
		125,000
Current accounts – Lyle	5,000	
Tate	6,000	
		11,000
		136,000

Activity 7

1   Debit   Partner's current account
    Credit   Purchases

2   Debit   Partner's current account
    Credit   Partner's drawings account

3   Debit   Appropriation account
    Credit   Partners' current accounts

4   It is the excess of the value of the partnership as a whole over the value of its net assets.

5   No, it is not usually recorded as a permanent asset. It is normally accounted for, and then immediately removed from the accounting records, when accounting for the admission or retirement of a partner.

8 Test your knowledge

 Workbook Activity 8

Low, High and Broad

Low, High and Broad are in partnership sharing profits and losses in the ratio 2:2:1 respectively. Interest is credited on partners' capital account balances at the rate of 5% per annum.

High is the firm's sales manager and for his specialised services he is to receive a salary of £800 per annum.

During the year ended 30 April 20X1 the profit for the year of the firm was £6,200 and the partners' drawings were as follows:

	£
Low	1,200
High	800
Broad	800

On 31 October 20X0 the firm agreed that Low should withdraw £1,000 from his capital account and that Broad should subscribe a similar amount to his capital account.

The credit balances on the partners' accounts at 1 May 20X0 were as follows:

	Capital accounts £	Current accounts £
Low	8,000	640
High	7,000	560
Broad	6,000	480

Required:

(a) Prepare a profit appropriation statement for the year ended 30 April 20X1.

(b) Prepare the partners' capital and current accounts for the year ended 30 April 20X1.

Workbook Activity 9

Curran and Edgar are in partnership as motor engineers.

The following figures were available after the preparation of the trial balance at 31 December 20X3.

Capital account (C)	£26,000
Capital account (E)	£20,000
Current account (C)	£6,100
Current account (E)	£5,200

Both current accounts showed credit balances

Drawings (C)	£16,250
Drawings (E)	£14,750

After the preparation of the statement of profit or loss, profit was determined as £42,100.

Profits are shared equally by the partners.

Task 1

Show the capital account for each partner updated to 1 January 20X4.

Task 2

Prepare the current account for each partner, balancing these off at the year end.

 Workbook Activity 10

Kate and Ed have been in partnership for a number of years sharing profits and losses equally.

On 1 March 20X3 it was decided to admit Rob to the partnership and he would introduce £30,000 of additional capital by payment into the partnership bank account.

Kate and Ed had capital balances on 1 March 20X3 of £50,000 and £40,000 respectively and the goodwill of the partnership was estimated to be £35,000.

After the admission of Rob, the partnership profits are to be shared with two fifths to Kate and Ed each and one fifth to Rob.

Write up the partners' capital accounts to reflect the admission of Rob.

Workbook Activity 11

Liam, Sam and Fred have been in partnership for a number of years sharing profits in the ratio of 3:2:1.

On 31 May 20X4 Liam retired from the partnership. He was due to be paid £20,000 on that date and the remainder is to remain as a loan to the partnership.

After Liam's retirement Sam and Fred are to share profits equally. The goodwill of the partnership at 31 May 20X4 was estimated to total £18,000.

The partners' capital and current account balances at 31 May 20X4 were as follows:

	£
Capital accounts	
Liam	50,000
Sam	40,000
Fred	30,000
Current accounts	
Liam	4,000
Sam	2,000
Fred	3,000

You are to write up the partners' capital accounts to reflect the retirement of Liam.

 Workbook Activity 12

Wilson and Bridget are in partnership running a toyshop. They have not had a successful year and have reported a loss of £56,000 in the year ended 30 September 20X8.

Their partnership agreement states the following:

• A salary of £9,000 for Wilson and £12,000 for Bridget.

• Interest on drawings above £10,000 in the year at 5%.

• Interest on capital at 10%.

• The balance of the profits to be shared equally.

Wilson has invested £30,000 in the business and Bridget £15,000. Wilson and Bridget took £14,000 and £8,000 respectively as drawings on 1 July 20X8.

What is Wilson's share of the loss?

Incomplete records

Introduction

The reconstruction of financial information from incomplete evidence is a key element of this unit when preparing accounts for a business.

There are a variety of techniques that can be used to reconstruct financial information when full accounting records are not available.

These include reconstruction of net asset totals, reconstruction of cash, bank, receivables and payables accounts and the use of mark-ups or margins in order to calculate missing accounting figures.

Each of these techniques will be considered in this chapter.

KNOWLEDGE

Describe the methods of constructing accounts from incomplete records (1.3)

Provide reasons for imbalances resulting from incorrect double entries (1.4)

Provide reasons for incomplete records arising from insufficient data and inconsistencies within the data provided (1.5)

SKILLS

Calculate opening and/or closing balances for capital and/or cash and bank balances using incomplete information (2.1), (2.2)

Prepare sales and purchase ledger control accounts, using these to correctly calculate sales, purchases and bank figures (2.3)

Calculate account balances using mark-ups and margins (2.4)

CONTENTS

1 What are incomplete records?
2 The net assets approach
3 Cash and bank account
4 Sales ledger control account and purchase ledger control account
5 Margins and mark-ups
6 Margins and mark-ups and incomplete records
7 Examination style questions
8 Summary

1   What are incomplete records?

1.1   Introduction

So far in this text we have been considering the accounting systems of sole traders and partnerships. They have all kept full accounting records consisting of primary records and a full set of ledger accounts, leading to a trial balance from which final accounts could be prepared.

In this chapter we will be considering businesses that do not keep full accounting records – incomplete records.

1.2   Limited records

Many businesses especially those of small sole traders or partnerships will only keep the bare minimum of accounting records. These may typically consist of:

- bank statements

- files of invoices sent to customers probably marked off when paid

- files of invoices received from suppliers marked off when paid

- files of bills marked off when paid

- till rolls

- a record of non-current assets owned.

From these records it will normally be possible to piece together the information required to prepare a statement of profit or loss and a statement of financial position but a number of techniques are required. These will all be covered in this chapter.

1.3   Destroyed records

In some situations, particularly in examinations, either the whole, or part, of the accounting records have been destroyed by fire, flood, thieves or computer failure. It will then be necessary to try to piece together the picture of the business from the information that is available.

1.4   Missing figures

A further element of incomplete records is that a particular figure or balance may be missing. Typically, inventory will be destroyed in accidents and drawings will be unknown. Incomplete records techniques can be used to find the missing amount or value as a balancing figure.

1.5　Techniques

In order to deal with these situations a number of specific accounting techniques are required and these will be dealt with in this chapter. They are:

- the net assets approach (based on the accounting equation)
- the cash and bank account
- receivables and payables control accounts
- mark-ups and margins.

2　The net assets approach

2.1　Introduction

The net assets approach is used in a particular type of incomplete records situation. This is where there are no detailed records of the transactions of the business during the accounting period. This may be due to the fact that they have been destroyed or that they were never kept in the first place. The only facts that can be determined are the net assets at the start of the year, the net assets at the end of the year and some details about the capital of the business.

2.2　The accounting equation

We have come across the accounting equation in earlier chapters when dealing with the statement of financial position.

The basic accounting equation is that:

Net assets　　　　　　　=　Capital

Remember that net assets = business assets – business liabilities

This can be expanded to:

Increase in net assets　=　Capital introduced + profit – drawings

This is important: any increase in the net assets of the business must be due to the introduction of new capital and/or the making of profit less drawings.

2.3 Using the accounting equation

If the opening net assets of the business can be determined and also the closing net assets then the increase in net assets is the difference.

Therefore if any capital introduced is known together with any drawings made by the owner, then the profit for the period can be deduced.

Alternatively if the profit and capital introduced are known then the drawings can be found as the balancing figure.

Example

Archibald started a business on 1 January 20X1 with £2,000. On 31 December 20X1 the position of the business was as follows:

	£
It owned	
Freehold lock–up shop, at cost	4,000
Shop fixtures and equipment, at cost	500
Inventory of goods bought for resale, at cost	10,300
Debts owing by customers	500
Cash in till	10
Cash at bank	150
It owed	
Mortgage on shop premises	3,000
Payables for goods	7,000
Accrued mortgage interest	100

Archibald had drawn £500 for personal living expenses.

The shop fixtures are to be depreciated by £50 and certain goods in inventory which had cost £300 can be sold for only £50.

No records had been maintained throughout the year.

You are required to calculate the profit earned by Archibald's business in the year ended 31 December 20X1.

Solution

This sort of question is answered by calculating the net assets at the year-end as follows:

Net assets at 31 December 20X1

	Cost £	Depreciation £	CV £
Non-current assets			
Freehold shop	4,000	–	4,000
Fixtures and fittings	500	50	450
	4,500	50	4,450

Current assets

Inventory at lower of cost and net realisable value (10,300 – 300 + 50)		10,050
Trade receivables		500
Cash and bank balances (150 + 10)		160
		10,710

Current liabilities

Trade payables	7,000		
Mortgage interest	100		
		(7,100)	
			3,610
			8,060
Mortgage			(3,000)
Net assets			5,060

The profit is now calculated from the accounting equation.

Note that the opening net assets will be the cash paid into the bank when the business was started on 1 January 20X1.

Change in net assets during the year = Profit plus capital introduced in year less drawings

£5,060 – 2,000 = Profit + Nil – 500

£3,060 = Profit – 500

Therefore, profit = £3,560

Archibald's statement of financial position is made up of the above together with the bottom half which can be established after calculating the profit, i.e.

	£
Capital	2,000
Profit (balancing figure)	3,560
	5,560
Drawings	(500)
	5,060

As you can see, the 'incomplete records' part of the question is concerned with just one figure. The question is really about the preparation of the statement of financial position.

Activity 1

The net assets of a business at the start of the year were £14,600. At the end of the year the net assets were £17,300. During the year the owner had paid in £2,000 of additional long term capital and withdrew £10,000 from the business for living expenses.

What is the profit of the business?

3 Cash and bank account

3.1 Introduction

In this section we must be quite clear about the distinction between cash and bank accounts.

 Definition

Cash is the amount of notes and coins in a till or in the petty cash box.

 Definition

The bank account is the amount held in the current account or cheque account of the business.

If the opening and closing balances of cash and bank are known together with most of the movements in and out, then, if there is only one missing figure this can be found as the balancing figure.

3.2 Cash account

When dealing with incomplete records a cash account deals literally with cash either from the petty cash box or more usually from the till in a small retail business. If the opening balance and the closing balance of cash is known then provided there is only one missing figure this can be determined from the summarised cash account.

Example

Henry's sales are all for cash. During the year he:

- banked £50,000

- paid wages of £5,000 out of the till, and

- paid expenses in cash of £10,000.

There were no opening or closing cash balances.

What were Henry's sales?

Solution

Working cash account

	£		£
Cash sales (bal fig)	65,000	Bank	50,000
		Wages	5,000
		Expenses	10,000
	_____		_____
	65,000		65,000
	_____		_____

The rationale is that if £65,000 of cash was taken out of the till for various purposes then £65,000 must have come in.

 Activity 2

Henrietta runs a milliner's shop making all her sales for cash. You ascertain the following information:

	£
Cash in the till at the beginning of the year	50
Cash in the till at the end of the year	75
Bingo winnings put into the till	500
Bankings	15,000
Cash wages	1,000
Cash expenses	5,000

Complete the ledger account below to establish Henrietta's sales during the year.

Working cash account

	£		£
	———		———
	———		———

3.3 Bank account

The same ideas can be applied to the bank account – if the opening and closing balances and all of the transactions except one are known then this missing figure can be found. In practice this may not be required though as bank statements should show all the necessary details.

Note that the double entry for bankings is

Dr Bank account

Cr Cash account

 Example

Henry writes cheques only for his own use. He knows that his bankings were £50,000.

The opening and closing bank balances were £10,000 and £40,000 respectively. What were his drawings?

Solution

Working bank account

	£		£
Balance b/d	10,000	Drawings (bal fig)	20,000
Bankings	50,000	Balance c/d	40,000
	———		———
	60,000		60,000
	———		———
Balance b/d	40,000		

The bankings are the amount paid out of the till and into the bank account. Therefore they must be a debit entry in the bank account.

3.4 Combined cash and bank account

In examinations it is often easier to combine the cash and bank accounts into one ledger account with a column for cash and a column for bank.

In the case of Henry this would be written as:

Working cash and bank account						
	Cash	Bank			Cash	Bank
	£	£			£	£
Balance b/d		10,000	Drawings (bal fig)			20,000
Bankings		50,000	Bankings		50,000	
Cash sales (bal fig)	65,000		Wages		5,000	
			Expenses		10,000	
			Balance c/d			40,000
	——	——			——	——
	65,000	60,000			65,000	60,000
	——	——			——	——

The key figure here is the bankings. If the bankings were paid into the bank account then they must have come out of the till or cash account.

In examinations you may only be given the bankings figure from the bank statement – this will show the amount paid into the bank account. You must then ensure that you make this entry not only as a debit in the bank column but also as a credit in the cash column.

4   Sales ledger control account and purchase ledger control account

4.1 Introduction

In many incomplete records situations you will find that the figures for sales and purchases are missing.

A technique for finding these missing figures is to recreate the receivables and payables accounts in order to find the missing figures as balancing figures.

The sales ledger control account and the purchase ledger control account are used to find the missing figures.

4.2 Sales ledger control account

Firstly a reminder of what is likely to be in a sales ledger control account is below:

Sales ledger control account

	£		£
Opening balance	X	Receipts from customers	X
Sales (per sales day book)	X	Sales returns	X
		Irrecoverable debts	X
		Discounts allowed	X
		Contra with PLCA	X
		Closing balance	X
	X		X

If the opening and closing receivables are known, together with the receipts from customers and details of any irrecoverable debts then the sales figure can be found as the balancing figure.

 Example

A business has receivables at the start of the year of £4,220 and at the end of the year receivables of £4,870.

During the year customers paid a total of £156,350 and one debt of £1,000 was irrecoverable.

What were the sales for the year?

Solution

Sales ledger control account

	£		£
Opening balance	4,220	Receipts from customers	156,350
		Irrecoverable debt written off	1,000
Sales (bal fig)	158,000	Closing balance	4,870
	162,220		162,220

The sales figure of £158,000 can be deduced from this account as the balancing figure.

4.3 Purchase ledger control account

The purchase ledger control account works in the same way as a potential working for finding the purchases figure.

Purchase ledger control account			
	£		£
Payments to suppliers	X	Opening balance	X
Discount received	X	Purchases	X
Purchase returns	X		
Contra with SLCA	X		
Closing balance	X		
	X		X

Example

Dominic paid his payables £5,000 during a period.

At the beginning of the period he owed £1,500 and at the end he owed £750.

What were his purchases for the period?

Solution

Purchase ledger control account			
	£		£
Cash	5,000	Balance b/d	1,500
Balance c/d	750	Purchases (bal fig)	4,250
	5,750		5,750
		Balance b/d	750

4.4 Cash, bank, receivables and payables

In many incomplete records questions you will need to combine the techniques learnt so far.

You may need to use the cash and bank account in order to determine the receipts from customers and then transfer this amount to the sales ledger control account in order to find the sales figure.

Example

Andrea does not keep a full set of accounting records but she has been able to provide you with some information about her opening and closing balances for the year ended 31 December 20X1.

	1 January 20X1 £	31 December 20X1 £
Inventory	5,227	4,892
Trade receivables	6,387	7,221
Trade payables	3,859	4,209
Bank	1,448	1,382
Cash	450	300

You have also been provided with a summary of Andrea's payments out of her bank account:

	£
Payments to trade payables	48,906
Purchase of new car	12,000
Payment of expenses	14,559

Andrea also tells you that she has taken £100 per week out of the till in cash in order to meet her own expenses.

Calculate sales, purchases, cost of sales and gross profit for Andrea for the year ended 31 December 20X1.

Solution

Step 1

Open up ledger accounts for cash and bank, receivables and payables and enter the opening and closing balances given.

Cash and bank

	Cash £	Bank £		Cash £	Bank £
Opening balance	450	1,448	Closing balance	300	1,382

Sales ledger control account

	£		£
Opening balance	6,387	Closing balance	7,221

Purchase ledger control account

	£		£
Closing balance	4,209	Opening balance	3,859

Step 2

Enter the payments from the bank account in the credit column of the bank account and complete the double entry for the payable's payment.

Cash and bank

	Cash £	Bank £		Cash £	Bank £
Opening balance	450	1,448	Payables		48,906
			Car		12,000
			Expenses		14,559
			Closing balance	300	1,382

Purchase ledger control account

	£		£
Bank	48,906	Opening balance	3,859
Closing balance	4,209		

Step 3

Find the balancing figure in the bank account as this is the amount of money paid into the bank in the period. If it was paid into the bank it must have come out of the till therefore enter the same figure as a credit in the cash account.

Cash and bank

	Cash	Bank		Cash	Bank
Opening balance	450	1,448	Payables		48,906
Bankings (bal fig)		75,399	Car		12,000
			Expenses		14,559
			Bankings	75,399	
			Closing balance	300	1,382
		76,847			76,847

Step 4

Enter the drawings into the cash account (assume a 52-week year unless told otherwise).

Cash and bank

	Cash £	Bank £		Cash £	Bank £
Opening balance	450	1,448	Payables		48,906
Bankings (bal fig)		75,399	Car		12,000
			Expenses		14,559
			Bankings	75,399	
			Drawings	5,200	
			Closing balance	300	1,382
		76,847			76,847

Step 5

Balance the cash account – the missing figure is the amount of receipts from customers – this is a debit in the cash account and a credit in the sales ledger control account.

Cash and bank

	Cash £	Bank £		Cash £	Bank £
Opening balance	450	1,448	Payables		48,906
Bankings (bal fig)		75,399	Car		12,000
			Expenses		14,559
			Bankings	75,399	
			Drawings	5,200	
Receipts – receivables (bal fig)	80,449		Closing balance	300	1,382
	80,899	76,847		80,899	76,847

Sales ledger control account

	£		£
Opening balance	6,387	Receipts from customers	80,449
		Closing balance	7,221

The receipts figure of £80,449 is not technically all from receivables since some may be for cash sales; however as the sales ledger control account is only a working account designed to find the total sales this distinction is unimportant.

Step 6

Find the sales and purchases figures as the missing figures in the receivables and payables account.

Sales ledger control account

	£		£
Opening balance	6,387	Receipts from customers	80,449
Sales (bal fig)	81,283	Closing balance	7,221
	87,670		87,670

Purchase ledger control account

	£		£
Bank	48,906	Opening balance	3,859
Closing balance	4,209	Purchases (bal fig)	49,256
	53,115		53,115

Step 7

Prepare the Trading account

	£	£
Revenue		81,283
Less: cost of sales		
Opening inventory	5,227	
Purchases	49,256	
	54,483	
Less: closing inventory	(4,892)	
		(49,591)
Gross profit		31,692

In this example we dealt with all four accounts – cash, bank, receivables and payables – simultaneously in order to show how the double entry works between the four working accounts.

However in examinations you will be prompted to work through the situation step by step. So, this same example might be approached in the examination as follows:

Task 1

Calculate the amount of cash received from customers from sales.

This will come from the cash and bank account workings. Cash and bank.

Cash and bank

	Cash £	Bank £		Cash £	Bank £
Opening balance	450	1,448	Payables		48,906
Bankings (bal fig)		75,399	Car		12,000
			Expenses		14,559
			Bankings	75,399	
			Drawings	5,200	
Receipts – receivables (bal fig)	80,449		Closing balance	300	1,382
	80,899	76,847		80,899	76,847

Cash from customers for sales = £80,449

Task 2

Determine the sales for the period.

This will come from the working sales ledger control account.

Sales ledger control account

	£		£
Opening balance	6,387	Receipts from customers	80,449
Sales (bal fig)	81,283	Closing balance	7,221
	87,670		87,670

Sales = £81,283

Task 3

Determine the purchases for the period.

This will come from the working purchase ledger control account.

Purchase ledger control account

	£		£
Bank	48,906	Opening balance	3,859
Closing balance	4,209	Purchases (bal fig)	49,256
	53,115		53,115

Purchases = £49,256

Task 4

Calculate the gross profit for the period.

This will come from the statement of profit or loss.

	£	£
Revenue		81,283
Less: cost of sales		
Opening inventory	5,227	
Purchases	49,256	
	54,483	
Less: closing inventory	(4,892)	
		(49,591)
Gross profit		31,692

Gross profit = £31,692

5 Margins and mark-ups

5.1 Introduction

The final technique that you may be required to use is that of dealing with margins and mark-ups. This is often useful when dealing with the records of a retailer and is a useful method of reconstructing missing figures.

5.2 Cost structure

The key to dealing with mark-ups and margins is in setting up the cost structure of the sales of an organisation from the information given in the question.

 Definition

A cost structure is the relationship between the selling price of goods, their cost and the gross profit earned in percentage terms.

Example

An item is sold for £150 and it originally cost £100. We need to set up the cost structure for this sale.

Solution

	£
Revenue	150
Cost of sales	100
Gross profit	50

The cost structure, in percentage terms, can be set up in one of two ways.

(i)   Assume that cost of sales represents 100% therefore the cost structure would be:

	£	%
Revenue	150	150
Cost of sales	100	100
Gross profit	50	50

We can now say that this sale gives a gross profit percentage of 50% on cost of sales.

(ii)   Assume that revenue represents 100% therefore the cost structure would be:

	£	%
Revenue	150	100
Cost of sales	100	$66^2/_3$
Gross profit	50	$33^1/_3$

We can now say that this sale gives a gross profit percentage of $33^1/_3$% on sales.

5.3 The difference between a mark-up and a margin

If it is cost of sales that is 100% then this is known as a mark-up on cost. Therefore in the previous example the sale would be described as having a mark-up on cost of 50%.

If it is revenue that is 100% then this is known as a sales margin. In the previous example the sale would be described as having a gross profit margin of $33^1/_3$%.

 Example

Calculate the cost of goods which have been sold for £1,200 on which a gross profit margin of 25% has been achieved.

Solution

Step 1

Work out the cost structure.

The phrase 'gross profit margin' means 'gross profit on sales'. Following the rule above we therefore make revenue equal to 100%. We know the gross profit is 25%; therefore the cost of sales must be 75%.

	%
Revenue	100
Less: cost of sales	75
Gross profit	25

Step 2

Work out the missing figure, in this case 'cost of sales'.

	£	%
Revenue	1,200	100
Cost of sales	?	75
Gross profit	?	25

Cost of goods sold = 75% of revenue

$$= \frac{75}{100} \times 1,200 = £900$$

Therefore gross profit = £300 (£1,200 – £900)

Example

Calculate the cost of goods which have been sold for £1,200 on which a mark-up on cost of sales of 25% has been achieved.

Solution

Step 1

The cost structure

The fact that the gross profit here is on cost of sales rather than sales as above makes all the difference. When we construct the 'cost structure', cost of sales will be 100%; gross profit will be 25%, so that revenue must be 125%.

In other words:

	%
Revenue	125
Less: cost of sales	100
Gross profit	25

Step 2

Calculate the missing figure, again the cost of sales

	£	%
Revenue	1,200	125
Cost of sales	?	100
Gross profit	?	25

Cost of goods sold = $\dfrac{100}{125}$ of revenue

$= \dfrac{100}{125} \times 1,200 = £960$

Remember the rule – whatever the margin or mark-up is 'on' or 'of' must be 100%.

- If there is a margin on sales price then revenues are 100%.

- If there is a mark-up on cost then cost of sales are 100%.

Activity 3

(a)   Mark-up on cost of sales = 10%

Revenues were £6,160

Cost of sales =

(b)   Gross profit on revenues = 20%

Cost of sales was £20,000

Revenues =

(c)   Mark-up on cost of sales = 33%

Cost of sales was £15,000

Revenues =

(d)   Gross profit on revenues = 25%

Cost of sales was £13,200

Revenues =

(e)   Revenues were £20,000

Cost of sales was £16,000

Gross profit on revenues as a % =

Gross profit on cost of sales as a % =

6   Margins and mark-ups and incomplete records

6.1   Introduction

We will now look at how mark-ups and margins can be used in incomplete records questions. They can be a great help in finding missing revenue and cost of sales figures but a little practice is required in using them.

6.2   Calculating revenues

In a question if you have enough information to calculate cost of sales and you are given some information about the cost structure of the revenues then you will be able to calculate revenue.

In examination questions if the percentage mark-up or margin is given then you will need to use it – do not try to answer the question without using it as you will get the answer wrong!

Example

A business has purchases of £18,000 and opening and closing inventory of £2,000 and £4,000 respectively. The gross profit margin is always 25%.

What are the revenues for the period?

Solution

Step 1

Cost structure

As it is a gross profit margin this is a margin 'on' revenue and therefore revenues are 100%

	%
Revenue	100
Cost of sales	75
	——
Gross profit	25
	——

Step 2

Calculate cost of sales

	£
Opening inventory	2,000
Purchases	18,000
	———
	20,000
Less: closing inventory	(4,000)
	———
	16,000
	———

Step 3

Determine the revenue figure

$$£16,000 \times \frac{100}{75} = £21,333$$

Activity 4

You are given the following information relating to Clarence's business for the year ended 31 December 20X3.

Cash paid to trade payables was £9,000. Other assets and liabilities were:

	1 January £	31 December £
Payables	2,100	2,600
Inventory	1,800	1,600

Mark-up on cost of sales 20%

Task 1

Calculate the purchases for the year.

Task 2

Calculate the cost of sales for the year.

Task 3

Calculate the revenues for the year.

6.3 Calculating cost of sales, purchases or closing inventory

If you know the figure for revenue and you know about the cost structure then it is possible to find the total for cost of sales and then deduce any missing figures such as purchases or closing inventory.

 Example

A business had made sales in the month of £25,000. The business sells its goods at a mark-up of 20%. The opening inventory was £2,000 and the closing inventory was £3,000.

What were the purchases for the period?

Solution

Step 1

Cost structure

	%
Revenue	120
Cost of sales	100
Gross profit	20

Step 2

Determine cost of sales using the cost structure.

$$\text{Cost of sales} = £25{,}000 \times \frac{100}{120}$$

$$= £20{,}833$$

Step 3

Reconstruct cost of sales to find purchases

	£
Opening inventory	2,000
Purchases (bal fig)	21,833
	23,833
Less: closing inventory	(3,000)
Cost of sales	20,833

7 Examination style questions

7.1 Introduction

So far we have studied the techniques that you have to use to deal with incomplete records questions in the exam. Although the examiner may ask any style of question, the examiner tends to ask questions in a particular way – leading you through the question a bit at a time and telling you what you have to calculate next. We shall now see how these questions might appear in the exam.

Example

John is a sole trader and prepares his accounts to 30 September 20X8. The summary of his bank account is as follows.

	£		£
Balance b/d 1 Oct 20X7	15,000	Stationery	2,400
Receipts from receivables	74,865	General expenses	4,300
		Rent	4,500
		Payments to suppliers	27,000
		Drawings	24,000
		Balance at 30 Sept 20X8	27,665
	89,865		**89,865**

Receivables at 1 October 20X7 were 24,000 and at 30 September 20X8 were 30,000.

Payables at 1 October 20X7 were 17,500 and at 30 September 20X8 were 23,000.

Rent was paid at £1,500 per quarter, and the rent had not been paid for the final quarter to 30 September 20X8.

During September 20X8 a payment of £300 was made for electricity which covered the period 1 August 20X8 to 31 October 20X8. Electricity is included in general expenses.

Task 1

Calculate the capital at 1 October 20X7.

Task 2

Prepare the sales ledger control account for the year ended 30 September 20X8, showing credit sales as the balancing figure.

Sales ledger control account

	£		£

Task 3

Prepare the purchases ledger control account for the year ended 30 September 20X8, showing credit purchases as the balancing figure.

Purchases ledger control account

	£		£

Task 4

Prepare the rent account for the year ended 30 September 20X8.

Rent account

	£		£

Task 5

Prepare the general expenses account for the year ended 30 September 20X8.

General expenses account

	£		£

Task 6

Prepare a trial balance at 30 September 20X8

Solution

Task 1

Capital at 1 October 20X7 = net assets at 1 October 20X7

Net assets at 1 October 20X7:	£
Bank	15,000
Receivables	24,000
Payables	(17,500)
	―――――
Net assets	21,500 = capital at 1 October 20X7
	―――――

Tutorial note. Remember that capital equals net assets. You therefore have to list all the assets and liabilities at the start of the year to find the net assets and therefore the capital.

Task 2

Sales ledger control account

	£		£
Balance b/d 1 Oct 20X7	24,000	Cash from receivables	74,865
Credit sales (bal fig)	80,865	Balance c/d 30 Sept 20X8	30,000
	―――――		―――――
	104,865		104,865
	―――――		―――――

Task 3

Purchases ledger control account

	£		£
Paid to payables	27,000	Balance b/d 1 Oct 20X7	17,500
Balance c/d 30 Sept 20X8	23,000	Purchases (bal fig)	32,500
	―――――		―――――
	50,000		50,000
	―――――		―――――

Task 4

Rent account

	£		£
Cash paid	4,500	Profit or loss	6,000
Balance c/d	1,500		
	———		———
	6,000		6,000
	———		———

Tutorial note. The £1,500 rent that has not been paid for the final quarter is an accrual – it is brought down into the next period as a credit balance as it is money owed by the business.

Task 5

General expenses account

	£		£
Cash paid	4,300	Profit or loss	4,200
		Balance c/d (1/3 × £300)	100
	———		———
	4,300		4,300
	———		———

Tutorial note. Of the £300 paid in September 20X8, £100 is for the month of October 20X8 – it is therefore a prepayment and is carried forward as an asset – a debit balance

Task 6

Trial balance as at 30 September 20X8

	£	£
Capital at 1 October 20X7		21,500
Bank	27,665	
Revenue		80,865
Sales ledger control a/c	30,000	
Purchases	32,500	
Purchases ledger control a/c		23,000
Accrual – rent		1,500
Prepayment – general expenses	100	
Stationery	2,400	
Rent (P&L)	6,000	
General expenses (P&L)	4,200	
Drawings	24,000	
	———	———
	126,865	126,865
	———	———

7.2   Another example

In many examination questions you will be required to use the incomplete records techniques to determine missing figures. We have already looked at finding revenue, cost of sales, purchases and closing or opening inventory. The final common missing figure is that of the owner's drawings.

Often the owner of a business will not keep a record of exactly how much has been taken out of the business especially if money tends to be taken directly from the till.

In examination questions if you are told that the owner's drawings were, for example, approximately £35 each week then this figure can be used as the actual drawings figure.

However if the question states that drawings were between £25 and £45 per week you cannot take an average figure; you must use incomplete records techniques to find the drawings figure as the balancing figure.

 Example

Simone runs a television and video shop.

All purchases are made on credit.

Sales are a mixture of cash and credit.

For the year ended 31 December 20X8, the opening and closing payables, receivables and inventory were:

	1.1.X8	21.12.X8
	£	£
Payables	11,000	11,500
Receivables	12,000	11,800
Inventory	7,000	10,000

Her mark-up is 20% on cost.

The payments for purchases are posted to the bank account and the purchase ledger control account.

All cash and cheques are posted to the cash account and sales ledger control account. Surplus cash and cheques are then paid into the bank.

A summary of her business bank account for the year ended 31 December 20X8 is as follows.

Bank account

	£		£
Balance b/d 1/1/X8	12,500	Payments to suppliers	114,000
Cash and cheques banked	121,000	Rent and rates	10,000
		Other expenses	4,000
		Balance c/d 31.12.X8	5,500
	133,500		133,500

The opening and closing cash balances were:

1/1/X8	31.12.X8
£120	£150

Simone made the following payments out of the till during the year:

	£
Petrol	400
Stationery	200

She also drew money out of the till for her personal use, but she has not kept a record of the amounts drawn.

Task 1

Prepare the purchase ledger control account

	£		£

Task 2

Calculate the cost of sales using the following proforma

£

Opening inventory

Purchases

_____

Closing inventory

_____

Cost of sales

_____

Task 3

Calculate revenue for the year using the following proforma and the details of the mark up given in the question.

£   %

Revenue

Cost of sales

_____

Gross profit

_____

Task 4

Prepare the sales ledger control account

	£		£

Task 5

Complete the cash account given below where drawings will be the balancing figure

Cash account

	£		£
Balance b/d		Petrol	
Receipts – receivables		Stationery	
		Bankings – to bank a/c	
		Drawings	
		Balance c/d	

Solution

Task 1

Calculation of purchases

Purchase ledger control account

	£		£
Bank account	114,000	Balance b/d	11,000
Balance c/d	11,500	Purchases (bal fig)	114,500
	———		———
	125,500		125,500
	———		———

Task 2

Calculation of cost of sales

	£
Opening inventory	7,000
Purchases (Task 1)	114,500
	———
	121,500
Closing inventory	(10,000)
	———
	111,500
	———

Task 3

Calculation of sales

	£	%
Revenue ($\frac{120}{100} \times 111{,}500$)	133,800	120
Cost of sales (Task 2)	111,500	100
Gross profit	22,300	20

Task 4

Sales ledger control account

	£		£
Balance b/d	12,000	Receipts (bal fig)	134,000
Revenue (Task 3)	133,800	Balance c/d	11,800
	145,800		145,800

Task 5

Drawings

Cash account

	£		£
Balance b/d	120	Petrol	400
Receipts – receivables	134,000	Stationery	200
		Bankings	121,000
		Drawings (bal fig)	12,370
		Balance c/d	150
	134,120		134,120

Take care with the order in which you work.

- As a mark-up is given you will need to use it – you have enough information to determine purchases and cost of sales therefore use the mark-up to calculate revenue.

- Make sure that you enter these sales into the sales ledger control account on the debit side – even though some are for cash rather than on credit they should all be entered into the receivables account as you are only using it as a vehicle for calculating the total revenue.

- Once sales have been entered into the receivables account the only missing figure is the cash received – this should be then entered into the cash account as a debit.

- Finally once all of the cash payments are entered as credits the balancing figure on the credit side of the cash account will be the drawings.

 Activity 5

Ignatius owns a small wholesale business and has come to you for assistance in the preparation of his accounts for the year ended 31 December 20X4.

For the year ended 31 December 20X4 no proper accounting records have been kept, but you establish the following information:

(1) A summary of Ignatius's bank statements for the year to 31 December 20X4 is as follows:

	£		£
Opening balance	1,870	Payments to suppliers	59,660
Receipts from credit customers	12,525	Rent – one year	4,000
Cash banked	59,000	Rates – year beginning 1.4.X4	2,000
		Other administration costs	1,335
		Selling costs	1,940
		Equipment – bought 1.1.X4	800
			69,735
		Closing balance	3,660
	73,395		73,395

(2) Credit sales for the year, as shown by a summary of copy invoices, totalled £12,760.

(3) No record has been kept by Ignatius of cash sales or his personal drawings, in cash. It is apparent, however, that all sales are on the basis of a 33$\frac{1}{3}$% mark-up on cost.

(4) Apart from drawings, cash payments during the year have been:

	£
Payments to suppliers	755
Sundry expenses	155
Wages	3,055

The balance of cash in hand at 31 December 20X4 is estimated at £20, and it is known that £12 was in hand at the beginning of the year.

(5) At the year-end, closing inventory, valued at cost, was £5,375 (31 December 20X3 £4,570) and payables for goods bought for resale amounted to £4,655.

(6) At 31 December 20X3 payables for goods bought for resale amounted to 3,845.

Task 1

Calculate the purchases for the year

Purchase ledger control account

	£		£
	___		___
	___		___

Task 2

Calculate the cost of sales for the year

	£
Opening inventory 1.1.X4	
Purchases	
	___
Inventory 31.12.X4	
	___
Cost of sales	
	___

Task 3

Calculate total revenue for the year

Revenue = (workings)

Cost structure

Cost of sales   =

Mark-up   =

Therefore revenue =

Task 4

Calculate the cash sales for the year

£

_____

Cash sales

_____

Task 5

Prepare calculations to determine the owner's drawings for the year.

Enter the cash sales in the cash account. This will give drawings as a balancing figure. The cash account is reproduced here.

Cash account

	£		£
	_____		_____
	_____		_____

Activity 6

1   According to the accounting equation, what is an increase in net assets equal to? (Write your answer below.)

2   What is the double entry for bankings from the cash till to the bank account? (Circle as appropriate.)

   Debit   **Revenue account / Bank account**

   Credit   **Cash account /Takings account**

3   The opening and closing receivables for a business were £1,000 and £1,500 and receipts from customers totalled £17,500. What were revenues? (Circle as appropriate.)

   Revenues are: **£17,500 / £17,000 / £18,000**

4   The opening and closing payables for a business were £800 and £1,200 with payments to suppliers totalling £12,200. What is the purchases figure? (Circle as appropriate.)

   Purchases are: **£12,600 / £12,200 / £11,800**

5   Goods costing £2,000 were sold at a mark up of 20%. What was the selling price? (Circle as appropriate.)

   Selling price is: **£2,500 / £2,400**

6   Goods costing £2,000 were sold with a margin of 20%. What was the selling price? (Circle as appropriate.)

   Selling price is: **£2,500 / £2,400**

7   Revenues were £24,000 and were at a margin of 25%. What is the figure for cost of sales? (Circle as appropriate.)

   Cost of sales is: **£18,000 / £6,000**

8   Revenues were £24,000 and were at a mark up of 25%. What is the figure for cost of sales? (Circle as appropriate.)

Cost of sales is   **£18,000 / £19,200**

9   Revenues for a business were £100,000 achieved at a margin of 40%. Opening inventory was £7,000 and purchases were £58,000. What is the figure for closing inventory? (Complete the proforma.)

	£	£
Revenues		
Less cost of goods sold		
Opening inventory		
Purchases		
Less closing inventory		
Gross profit		

10 Revenues for a business were £80,000 and they were sold at a mark up of 25%. Opening and closing inventory was £10,000 and £8,000 respectively. What is the purchase total? (Complete the pro forma.)

	£	£
Revenues		
Less cost of goods sold		
Opening inventory		
Purchases		
Less closing inventory		
Gross profit		

8 Summary

This chapter has covered all of the varying techniques that might be required to deal with an incomplete records problem in an examination.

The techniques are the net assets approach, cash and bank accounts, sales ledger control account and purchase ledger control account, plus use of mark-ups and margins.

Many of these questions will look formidable in an examination but they are all answerable if you think about all of these techniques that you have learnt and apply them to the particular circumstances of the question.

You will also find that the AAT style is to lead you through a question with small tasks prompting you to carry out the calculations in a particular order which makes the process more manageable.

Answers to chapter activities

 Activity 1

Increase in net assets	=	capital introduced	+ profit – drawings
(17,300 – 14,600)	=	2,000	+ profit – 10,000
2,700	=	2,000	+ profit – 10,000
Profit	=	£10,700	

 Activity 2

Working cash account

	£		£
Balance b/d	50	Bankings	15,000
Capital (Bingo)	500	Wages	1,000
Cash sales (bal fig)	20,525	Expenses	5,000
		Balance c/d	75
	21,075		21,075

The rationale is that £21,075 has been 'used' for bankings, expenses and providing a float to start the next period therefore £21,075 must have been received.

Of this 'receipt':

- £50 is from last period; and

- £500 is an injection of capital.

Therefore £20,525 must have been sales.

Activity 3

		%	£
(a)	Cost of sales	100	
	Add: mark–up	10	
	Therefore revenue	110	
	Therefore cost of sales	$^{100}/_{110}$ × £6,160	£5,600
(b)	Revenue	100	
	Less: gross profit	20	
	Therefore cost of sales	80	
	Therefore revenue	$^{100}/_{80}$ × £20,000	£25,000
(c)	Cost of sales	100	
	Add: mark–up	33	
	Therefore revenue	133	
	Therefore revenue	$^{133}/_{100}$ × £15,000	£19,950
(d)	Revenue	100	
	Less: gross profit	25	
	Therefore cost of sales	75	
	Therefore revenue	$^{100}/_{75}$ × £13,200	£17,600
(e)	Revenue	20,000	
	Less: cost of sales	16,000	
	Therefore gross profit	4,000	

$$\text{Gross profit on revenue} \quad \frac{4,000}{20,000} \times \frac{100}{1} = 20\%$$

$$\text{Gross profit on cost of sales} \quad \frac{4,000}{16,000} \times \frac{100}{1} = 25\%$$

Activity 4

Task 1

Calculate the figure for purchases.

Purchase ledger control account

	£		£
Cash	9,000	Balance b/d	2,100
Balance c/d	2,600	Purchases (bal fig)	9,500
	11,600		11,600

Note that we are constructing the total account, and producing the balancing figure which represents the purchases made during the year.

Remember the double-entry involved here. The cash of £9,000 will be a credit in the cash account. The purchases (£9,500) will be debited to the purchases account and transferred to the statement of profit or loss at the year-end:

Purchases account

	£		£
Purchase ledger control account	9,500	Statement of P & L	9,500

Task 2

Now complete the cost of sales

	£
Opening inventory	1,800
Purchases	9,500
	11,300
Less: closing inventory	(1,600)
Cost of sales	9,700

Task 3

Now you can work out the cost structure and revenue.

(a) Work out the cost structure.

The mark-up is arrived at by reference to the cost of sales. Thus, cost of sales is 100%, the mark-up is 20% and therefore the revenues are 120%:

	%
Revenue (balancing figure)	120
Less: Gross profit	20
Cost of sales	100

(b) Revenue $= \dfrac{120}{100} \times$ cost of sales

$\qquad = \dfrac{120}{100} \times £9,700$

$\qquad = £11,640$

Activity 5

Task 1

Calculate purchases

Purchase ledger control account

	£		£
Cash – payments to suppliers	755	Payables 1/1/X4	3,845
Bank – payments to suppliers	59,660	Purchases (balancing figure)	61,225
Payables 31.12.X4	4,655		
	65,070		65,070

Task 2

Calculate the cost of sales.

	£
Opening inventory 1.1.X4	4,570
Purchases	61,225
	65,795
Inventory 31.12.X4	(5,375)
Cost of sales	60,420

Task 3

Calculate total sales

Cost of structure

Cost of sales	=	100%
Mark-up	=	$33^1/_3\%$
Therefore sales	=	$133^1/_3\%$

$$\text{Sales} = \frac{\text{Cost of sales}}{100} \times 133^1/_3 = \frac{60,420}{100} \times 133^1/_3 = £80,560$$

Task 4

Calculate cash sales

	£
Total revenue	80,560
Less: credit sales (per question)	(12,760)
Therefore, cash sales	67,800

Task 5

Calculate drawings

Enter the cash sales in the cash account. This will give drawings as a balancing figure.

The cash account is reproduced here.

Cash account

	£		£
Balance 1.1.X4	12	Payments to suppliers	755
Receipts from cash sales	67,800	Other costs	155
		Wages	3,055
		Cash banked	59,000
		Drawings (balancing figure)	4,827
		Balance c/d	20
	67,812		67,812

Activity 6

1   Increase in net assets = capital introduced + profit – drawings

2   Debit   Bank account
    Credit   Cash account

3   £17,500 + 1,500 – £1,000   =   £18,000

4   £12,200 + £1,200 – £800   =   £12,600

5   £2,000 × 120/100   =   £2,400

6   £2,000 × 100/80   =   £2,500

7   £24,000 × 75/100   =   £18,000

8   £24,000 × 100/125   =   £19,200

9   Cost of sales = £100,000 × 60/100   =   £60,000
    Opening inventory + purchases   =   £65,000
    Closing inventory   =   £5,000

10 Cost of sales = £80,000 × 100/125   =   £64,000
    Purchases = £64,000 + £8,000 – £10,000 =   £62,000

9 Test your knowledge

 Workbook Activity 7

You work as a senior for a self-employed 'Licensed Accounting Technician' and Peter Ryan, the proprietor of a local shop trading in 'home brew products', is one of your clients.

The business trades under the name of Brew-By-Us.

The statement of financial position of the business at 31 May 20X0 was:

	Cost £	Depreciation £	CV £
Non-current assets			
Shop lease	10,000	2,000	8,000
Fixtures and fittings	3,000	1,200	1,800
	13,000	3,200	9,800
Current assets			
Inventory		3,500	
Rent and rates prepaid		950	
		4,450	
Less current liabilities			
Trade payables		1,200	
Heat and light accrued		200	
Bank overdraft		750	
		2,150	
Net current assets			2,300
Net assets			12,100
Financed by			
Capital			12,100

All the business's sales are on a cash basis, and during the current year all the takings other than £10,400, used by Peter for his own personal needs, have been banked.

All payments for expenses have been made by cheque.

A summary of the bank transactions for the year ended 31 May 20X1 is as follows:

	£
Balance b/d	(750) overdrawn
Receipts	
Shop takings	49,560
	———
	48,810
	———
Payments	
Wages	3,850
Advertising	750
Payments to suppliers	36,200
Heat and light	1,060
Shop fixtures	2,000
Insurance	400
Rent and rates	5,400
Shop repairs	200
Bank charges and interest	320
	———
	50,180
	———
Balance 31 May 20X1	(1,370) overdrawn
	———

Additional information for the year ended 31 May 20X1 is provided:

- Closing inventory has been valued at £3,800.

- Rent and rates of £1,050 were prepaid.

- Heat and light of £260 was accrued.

- £1,500 was owed to payables.

- Cash discounts received from suppliers in the year were £1,280.

- Depreciation is to be charged, straight line 10% on the lease and 20% fixtures and fittings. A full year's depreciation is to be charged in the year of acquisition.

Required:

(a) Determine the sales for the year.

(b) Determine the purchases for the year.

(c) Show accounts for heat and light and rent and rates, to determine the charge for the current year.

(d) Prepare a statement of profit or loss for the year ended 31 May 20X1, and a statement of financial position at that date.

 Workbook Activity 8

Diane Kelly has been employed for several years supplying cleaning materials to schools, restaurants, public houses and industrial units.

She operates an incomplete system of accounting records for her business, from which the following information is available.

1   **Assets and liabilities**

	1 June 20X0 £	31 May 20X1 £
Warehouse fittings (CV)	8,000	?
Van (at cost)	–	6,500
Inventory	10,000	16,000
Trade receivables	16,000	19,000
Trade payables	15,000	20,000
Rates prepaid	1,200	1,600
Accruals		
Telephone	400	500
Heat and light	300	500

2 Bank account summary for the year

	£	£
Balance at 1 June 20X0		9,800
Receipts		
Receivables	79,000	
Cash sales banked	7,700	
Proceeds of sale of caravan	2,500	89,200
Payments		
Payables	70,000	
Purchase of van	6,500	
Heat and light	1,800	
Office expenses	2,600	
Rent and rates	4,200	
Telephone	1,200	
Wages	9,800	
Van expenses	1,200	
Insurance	800	98,100
		———
Balance at 31 May X1		900
		———

Notes

- The caravan was Diane's own personal property.

- All non-current assets are depreciated on the reducing balance basis; a rate of 20% should be applied.

- The van was acquired on 1 June 20X0.

- During the year cash discounts of £1,100 had been allowed and £1,800 had been received.

- Diane paid sundry office expenses of £420 and used £15,600 for personal reasons – both amounts had been taken from the proceeds of cash sales.

- All the remaining cash had been banked.

Required:

(a) Determine the sales for the year.

(b) Determine the purchases for the year.

(c) Show accounts for rates, telephone and heat and light to determine the charge for the year.

(d) Prepare the statement of profit or loss for the year ended 31 May 20X1 and a statement of financial position at that date.

Workbook Activity 9

(a)   A business marks up its goods by 60%. Revenues are £200,000 for the year. What is the gross profit?

(b)   A business makes a 30% margin on its sales. Opening inventory is £40,000, closing inventory is £10,000 and purchases are £180,000. What is the amount for revenue?

 Workbook Activity 10

Data

A friend of Donald Johnson, Sheena Gordon, has been trading for just over 12 months as a dressmaker.

She has kept no accounting records at all, and she is worried that she may need professional help to sort out her financial position.

Knowing that Donald Johnson runs a successful business, Sheena Gordon approached him for advice. He recommended that you, his bookkeeper, should help Sheena Gordon.

You meet with Sheena Gordon and discuss the information that you require her to give you.

Sometime later, you receive a letter from Sheena Gordon providing you with the information that you requested, as follows:

(a)   She started her business on 1 October 20X2. She opened a business bank account and paid in £5,000 of her savings.

(b)   During October she bought the equipment and the inventory that she needed. The equipment cost £4,000 and the inventory of materials cost £1,800. All of this was paid for out of the business bank account.

(c) A summary of the business bank account for the 12 months ended 30 September 20X3 showed the following:

Bank

	£		£
Capital	5,000	Equipment	4,000
Cash banked	27,000	Purchases	1,800
		Purchases of materials	18,450
		General expenses	870
		Drawings	6,200
		Balance c/d	680
	32,000		32,000

(d) All of the sales are on a cash basis. Some of the cash is paid into the bank account while the rest is used for cash expenses. She has no idea what the total value of her sales is for the year, but she knows that from her cash received she has spent £3,800 on materials and £490 on general expenses. She took the rest of the cash not banked for her private drawings. She also keeps a cash float of £100.

(e) The gross profit margin on all sales is 50%.

(f) She estimates that all the equipment should last for five years. You therefore agree to depreciate it using the straight line method.

(g) On 30 September 20X3, the payables for materials amounted to £1,400.

(h) She estimates that the cost of inventory of materials that she had left at the end of the year was £2,200.

Task 10.1

Calculate the total purchases for the year ended 30 September 20X3.

Task 10.2

Calculate the total cost of sales for the year ended 30 September 20X3.

Task 10.3

Calculate revenue for the year ended 30 September 20X3.

Task 10.4

Show the entries that would appear in Sheena Gordon's cash account.

Task 10.5

Calculate the total drawings made by Sheena Gordon throughout the year.

Task 10.6

Calculate the figure for net profit for the year ended 30 September 20X3.

Workbook Activity 11

Fariah is a sole trader running an IT support business and prepares accounts to 31 December 20X8. The summary of her bank account is as follows.

	£		£
Balance b/d 1 Jan 20X8	25,000	Advertising	10,000
Receipts from receivables	80,000	General expenses	8,000
		Rent	9,000
		Payments to suppliers	10,000
		Drawings	36,000
		Balance at 31 Dec 20X8	32,000
	—————		—————
	105,000		**105,000**
	—————		—————

Receivables at 1 January 20X8 were £20,000 and at 31 December 20X8 were £30,000.

Payables at 1 January 20X8 were £13,000 and at 31 December 20X8 were £15,000.

All Fariah's sales are on credit. One of Fariah's receivables has been made bankrupt owing her £3,400. She wrote this debt off in November 20X8.

During December 20X8 a payment of £3,000 was made for insurance which covered the period 1 November 20X8 to 31 October 20X9. Insurance is included in general expenses.

Fariah depreciated her computers at 40% reducing balance. The CV of the computers at 1 January 20X8 was £4,600.

Task 11.1

Calculate the capital at 1 January 20X8.

Task 11.2

Prepare the journal that Fariah would have made in November 20X8 to record the write off of the irrecoverable debt.

Journal

Account name	Dr (£)	Cr (£)
Narrative		

Task 11.3

Prepare the sales ledger control account for the year ended 31 December 20X8, showing credit sales as the balancing figure.

Sales ledger control account

	£		£

Task 11.4

Prepare the purchases ledger control account for the year ended 31 December 20X8, showing credit purchases as the balancing figure.

Purchases ledger control account

	£		£

Task 11.5

Prepare the general expenses account for the year ended 31 December 20X8.

General expenses account

	£		£

Task 11.6

Calculate the depreciation that Fariah will provide for the year ended 31 December 20X8.

Task 11.7

Prepare the journal that Fariah will make at the year end to record depreciation.

Account name	Dr (£)	Cr (£)
Narrative		

Task 11.8

Prepare a trial balance at 31 December 20X8. The trial balance should show the computers at their carrying value (not cost less accumulated depreciation).

WORKBOOK ACTIVITIES
ANSWERS

Workbook Activities Answers

1 Preparation of accounts for a sole trader

Workbook Activity 5

David Pedley

Statement of profit or loss for the year ended 31 December 20X8

	£	£
Sales		28,400
Less: Returns		(200)
		28,200
Opening inventory		–
Purchases	16,100	
Less: Closing inventory	(2,050)	
Cost of sales		(14,050)
Gross profit		14,150
Salaries	4,162	
Rent and rates	2,130	
Insurance	174	
General expenses	1,596	
Total expenses		(8,062)
Profit for the year		6,088

Statement of financial position as at 31 December 20X8

	£	£
Non-current assets		
Motor van		1,700
Current assets		
Closing inventory	2,050	
Trade receivables	5,060	
Cash at bank	2,628	
Cash in hand	50	
	9,788	
Trade payables	(6,400)	
Net current assets		3,388
Net assets		5,088
Capital account		
Capital introduced		4,100
Profit for the year (per income statement)		6,088
Less: Drawings		(5,100)
Proprietor's funds		5,088

Workbook Activity 6

Karen Finch

Statement of profit or loss for the year ended 31 March 20X8

	£	£
Revenue (£17,314 + £4,256)		21,570
Purchases (£10,350 + £5,672)	16,022	
Closing inventory	(4,257)	
	————	(11,765)
		————
Gross profit		9,805
Assistant's salary plus bonus (£2,000 + £400)	2,400	
Electricity (£560 + £170)	730	
Rent and rates	1,100	
Postage and stationery	350	
Depreciation	1,000	
	————	
Total expenses		(5,580)
		————
Profit for the year		4,225
		————

Statement of financial position at 31 March 20X8

	£	£
Non-current assets		
Motor van at cost		4,000
Accumulated depreciation		(1,000)
		————
Carrying value		3,000
Current assets		
Inventory	4,257	
Trade receivables	4,256	
Cash (W1)	6,554	
	————	
	15,067	
	————	

Current liabilities		
Trade payables	5,672	
Accruals (400 + 170)	570	
	———	
	6,242	
	———	
Net current assets		8,825
		———
Net assets		11,825
		———
Capital		10,000
Capital introduced at 1 April 20X7		
Profit for the year	4,225	
Less Drawings	(2,400)	
	———	
Retained profit for the year		1,825
		———
Proprietors funds		11,825
		———

Working

(W1) Cash balance at 31 March 20X8

	£	£
Capital introduced at 1 April 20X7		10,000
Amounts received from customers		17,314
		———
		27,314
Salary of assistant	2,000	
Cash paid to suppliers	10,350	
Purchase of motor van	4,000	
Drawings	2,400	
Electricity	560	
Rent and rates	1,100	
Postage and stationery	350	
	———	
		20,760
		———
Cash balance at 31 March 20X8		6,554
		———

Workbook Activity 7

(a)   Ledger accounts

(i)

Closing inventory (I/S)

	£		£
Balance to income statement	3,060	Closing inventory SoFP	3,060

Closing inventory (SoFP)

	£		£
Closing inventory P&L	3,060	Balance c/d	3,060
	3,060		3,060
Balance b/d	3,060		

(ii)

Electricity

	£		£
Per trial balance	379	Profit or loss	423
Accrual	44		
	423		423

Rates

	£		£
Per trial balance	1,490	Profit or loss	1,175
		Prepayment	315
	1,490		1,490

Points to note:

- As regards electricity the accrual of £44 is shown on the statement of financial position as a current liability and increases the charge to profit or loss for electricity for expenses incurred but not yet paid.

- The rates prepayment of £315 is shown on the statement of financial position as a current asset and reduces the charge to profit or loss. This reflects the fact that some of the expense recorded relates to the next accounting year.

(b)

Elmdale

Statement of profit or loss for the year ended

31 December 20X8

	£	£
Revenue		21,417
Opening inventory	2,700	
Purchases	9,856	
	12,556	
Closing inventory	(3,060)	
Cost of sales		9,496
Gross profit		11,921
Rates	1,175	
Electricity	423	
Wages and salaries	3,704	
Sundry expenses	2,100	
Total expenses		7,402
Profit for the year		4,519

2 Partnership accounts

Workbook Activity 8

(a) **Profit appropriation statement – year ended 30 April 20X1:**

	Year ended 30 Apr 20X1 £	Total £
Profit for the year		6,200
Salaries		
Low	–	
High	(800)	
Broad	–	(800)
Interest on capital		
Six months to 31 Oct 20X0		
Low	(200)	
High	(175)	
Broad	(150)	(525)
Six months to 30 Apr 20X1		
Low	(175)	
High	(175)	
Broad	(175)	(525)
Profit available for distribution		4,350
Profit share		
Low	(1,740)	
High	(1,740)	
Broad	(870)	(4,350)
Balance		Nil

Summary of profit share for the year:

Low: £200 + £175 + £1,740 = £2,115

High: £800 + £175 + £175 + £1,740 = £2,890

Broad: £150 + £175 + £870 + £1,195

(b)

Capital accounts

	Low £	High £	Broad £		Low £	High £	Broad £
Cash	1,000	–	–	Balance b/d	8,000	7,000	6,000
Balance c/d	7,000	7,000	7,000	Cash			1,000
	8,000	7,000	7,000		8,000	7,000	7,000
				Balance b/d	7,000	7,000	7,000

Current accounts

	Low £	High £	Broad £		Low £	High £	Broad £
Drawings	1,200	800	800	Balance b/d	640	560	480
Balance c/d	1,555	2,650	875	Profit apportionment	2,115	2,890	1,195
	2,755	3,450	1,675		2,755	3,450	1,675
				Balance b/d	1,555	2,650	875

Workbook Activity 9

Capital account

	(C) £	(E) £		(C) £	(E) £
31 Dec Balance c/d	26,000	20,000	31 Dec Balance b/d	26,000	20,000
	26,000	20,000	01 Jan Balance b/d	26,000	20,000
			01 Jan Balance b/d	26,000	20,000

Current account

	(C) £	(E) £		(C) £	(E) £
31 Dec Drawings	16,250	14,750	Balance b/d	6,100	5,200
31 Dec Balance c/d	10,900	11,500	31 Dec Share of profit	21,050	21,050
	27,150	26,250		27,150	26,250
			01 Jan Balance b/d	10,900	11,500

Workbook Activity 10

Capital accounts

	Kate £	Ed £	Rob £		Kate £	Ed £	Rob £
				Balance b/d	50,000	40,000	
Goodwill	14,000	14,000	7,000	Goodwill	17,500	17,500	
Balance c/d	53,500	43,500	23,000	Bank			30,000
	67,500	57,500	30,000		67,500	57,500	30,000

Workbook Activity 11

Capital accounts

	Liam £	Sam £	Fred £		Liam £	Sam £	Fred £
				Balance b/d	50,000	40,000	30,000
				Current a/c	4,000		
Goodwill		9,000	9,000	Goodwill	9,000	6,000	3,000
Bank	20,000						
Loan	43,000						
Balance c/d		37,000	24,000				
	63,000	46,000	33,000		63,000	46,000	33,000

Workbook Activity 12

	Year ended 30 Sep 20X8 £	Total £
Loss for the year		(56,000)
Salaries		
Wilson	(9,000)	
Bridget	(12,000)	(21,000)
Interest on capital		
Wilson	(3,000)	
Bridget	(1,500)	(4,500)
Interest on drawings		
Wilson (£4,000 × 5% × 3/12)	50	
Bridget	–	50
Loss available for distribution		(81,450)
Loss share		
A	40,725	
B	40,725	81,450
Balance		Nil

Wilson's total share = £9,000 + £3,000 − £50 − £40,725 = **£28,775 loss.**

3 Incomplete records

✎ Workbook Activity 7

(a) Sales for the year

	£
Takings banked	49,560
Personal drawings	10,400
Total sales	59,960

(b) Purchases for the year

Purchase ledger control account

	£		£
31/5/X1 Payments	36,200	01/6/X0 Balance b/d	1,200
31/5/X1 Discounts	1,280	31/5/X1 Purchases (bal fig)	37,780
Balance c/d	1,500		
	38,980		38,980

(c)

Heat and light

	£		£
31/5/X1 Payments	1,060	01/6/X0 Balance b/d	200
31/5/X1 Balance c/d	260	31/5/X1 Profit or loss	1,120
	1,320		1,320
		01/6/X1 Balance b/d	260

Rent and rates

	£		£
01/6/X0 Balance b/d	950	31/5/X1 Balance c/d	1,050
31/5/X1 Payments	5,400		
		31/5/X1 Profit or loss	5,300
	6,350		6,350
01/6/X1 Balance b/d	1,050		

(d) **Statement of profit or loss of Peter Ryan trading as 'Brew-By Us' for the year ended 31 May 20X1**

	£	£
Revenue		59,960
Inventory at 1 June 20X0	3,500	
Add Purchases	37,780	
	41,280	
Less Inventory 31 May 20X1	3,800	
Cost of goods sold		37,480
Gross profit		22,480
Discounts received		1,280
Expenses		
Wages	3,850	
Advertising	750	
Heat and light	1,120	
Insurance	400	
Rent and rates	5,300	
Shop repairs	200	
Bank charges	320	
Depreciation		
Lease (10% × £10,000)	1,000	
Fixtures (20% × £5,000)	1,000	
Total expenses		13,940
Profit for the year		9,820

Statement of financial position as at 31 May 20X1

	Cost £	Depreciation £	CV £
Non-current assets			
Lease	10,000	3,000	7,000
Fixtures and fittings	5,000	2,200	2,800
	15,000	5,200	9,800
Current assets			
Inventory		3,800	
Prepayments		1,050	
		4,850	
Current liabilities			
Payables		1,500	
Accruals		260	
Bank overdraft		1,370	
		3,130	
Net current assets			1,720
Net assets			11,520
Capital		12,100	
Add Profit for year		9,820	
		21,920	
Less Drawings		10,400	
Proprietors funds			11,520

Workbook Activity 8

(a) Revenue for the year

Sales ledger control account

	£		£
01/6/X0 Balance b/d	16,000	31/5/X1 Bank	79,000
31/5/X1 Sales (bal fig)	83,100	31/5/X1 Discounts	1,100
		31/5/X1 Balance c/d	19,000
	99,100		99,100
01/6/X1 Balance b/d	19,000		

	£
Credit sales	83,100
Cash sales banked	7,700
Expenses paid by cash	420
Cash for personal use	15,600
Total revenue	106,820

(b) Purchases for the year

Purchase ledger control account

	£		£
31/5/X1 Payments	70,000	01/6/X0 Balance b/d	15,000
31/5/X1 Discounts	1,800	31/5/X1 (Purchases) bal fig	76,800
31/5/X1 Balance c/d	20,000		
	91,800		91,800

KAPLAN PUBLISHING

(c)

Rates account

	£		£
01/6/X0 Balance b/d	1,200	31/5/X1 Profit or loss	3,800
31/5/X1 Payments	4,200	31/5/X1 Balance c/d	1,600
	5,400		5,400
01/6/X1 Balance b/d	1,600		

Telephone account

	£		£
31/5/X1 Payments	1,200	01/6/X0 Balance b/d	400
31/5/X1 Balance c/d	500	31/5/X1 Profit or loss	1,300
	1,700		1,700
		01/6/X1 Balance b/d	500

Heat and light

	£		£
31/5/X1 Payments	1,800	01/6/X0 Balance b/d	300
31/5/X1 Balance c/d	500	31/5/X1 Profit or loss	2,000
	2,300		2,300
		01/6/X1 Balance b/d	500

(d)   Statement of profit or loss for year ended 31 May 20X1

	£	£
Revenue		106,820
Inventory – 1/6/X0	10,000	
Add: purchases	76,800	
	86,800	
Less: Inventory 31/5/X1	16,000	
Cost of sales		70,800
Gross profit		36,020
Discounts received		1,800
Expenses		
Heat and light	2,000	
Office expenses (2,600 + 420)	3,020	
Rent and rates	3,800	
Telephone	1,300	
Wages	9,800	
Vehicle expenses	1,200	
Insurance	800	
Depreciation		
Warehouse fittings	1,600	
Van	1,300	
Discounts allowed	1,100	
Total expenses		25,920
Profit for the year for year		11,900

Statement of financial position as at 31 May 20X1

	£	£
Non-current assets		
Warehouse fittings (8,000 – 1,600)		6,400
Van (6,500 – 1,300)		5,200
		11,600
Current assets		
Inventory	16,000	
Trade receivables	19,000	
Prepayment (rates)	1,600	
Cash at bank	900	
	37,500	
Current liabilities		
Trade payables	20,000	
Accruals (500 + 500)	1,000	
	21,000	
Net current assets		16,500
Net assets		28,100
Capital (W)		29,300
Add: capital introduced (caravan sale)		2,500
Add: profit for year		11,900
		43,700
Less: drawings		15,600
Proprietors funds		28,100

Working

The opening capital can be entered as the balancing figure on the statement of financial position. Alternatively it can be proved as follows:

	£
Fittings	8,000
Inventory	10,000
Receivables	16,000
Payables	(15,000)
Prepayments	1,200
Accruals	(700)
Bank	9,800
	29,300

Workbook Activity 9

(a)

	£	%
Revenue	200,000	160
Cost of sales		100
Gross profit ($\frac{60}{160} \times 200{,}000$)	75,000	60

	£	%
(b) Revenue = (($\frac{100}{70}$) × 210,000)	300,000	100
Cost of sales (see below)	210,000	70
Gross profit	90,000	30

Cost of sales	
Opening inventory	40,000
Purchases	180,000
Closing inventory	(10,000)
	210,000

Workbook Activity 10

Task 10.1

Total purchases

	£
Purchase of inventory bought in October	1,800
Purchases (bank)	18,450
Cash payments	3,800
Closing payables	1,400
	25,450

Task 10.2

Cost of sales

	£
Purchases	25,450
Less closing inventory	2,200
	23,250

Task 10.3

Sales for the year

If GP margin on sales is 50% then sales are £23,250 × $\dfrac{100}{50}$ = £46,500

Task 10.4

Cash account			
	£		£
Cash sales	46,500	Bankings	27,000
		Materials	3,800
		General expenses	490
		Drawings (bal fig)	15,110
		Float balance c/d	100
	46,500		46,500

Task 10.5

	£
Cash drawings (from Task 4)	15,110
Bank	6,200
	————
	21,310
	————

Task 10.6

	£
Gross profit	23,250
Less expenses:	
General expenses (870 + 490)	(1,360)
Depreciation (4,000 × 1/5)	(800)
	————
Profit for the year	21,090
	————

Workbook Activity 11

Task 11.1

Capital at 1 January 20X8

	£
Bank	25,000
Trade receivables	20,000
Computers	4,600
Trade payables	(13,000)
	————
Capital	36,600
	————

Tutorial note. Remember that capital equals net assets. You therefore have to list all the assets and liabilities at the start of the year to find the net assets and therefore the capital.

Task 11.2

Journal

Account name	Dr (£)	Cr (£)
Irrecoverable debt expense	3,400	
Sales ledger control account		3,400
Narrative	Being the irrecoverable debt	

Task 11.3

Sales ledger control account

	£		£
Balance b/d 1 Jan 20X8	20,000	Cash from receivables	80,000
		Irrecoverable debt	3,400
Credit sales (bal fig)	93,400	Balance c/d 31 Dec 20X8	30,000
	113,400		113,400

Task 11.4

Purchases ledger control account

	£		£
Paid to payables	10,000	Balance b/d 1 Jan 20X8	13,000
Balance c/d 31 Dec 20X8	15,000	Purchases (bal fig)	12,000
	25,000		25,000

Task 11.5

General expenses account

	£		£
Cash paid	8,000	Profit or loss	5,500
		Balance c/d	2,500
	8,000		8,000

Tutorial note. The £3,000 insurance covers 10 months of the following year – a prepayment of £3,000 × 10/12 = £2,500.

Task 11.6

Depreciation for the year ended 31 December 20X8

	£
CV at 1 January 20X8	4,600
Depreciation for the year at 40%	1,840
	——
	2,760
	——

Task 11.7

Journal

Account name	Dr (£)	Cr (£)
Depreciation expense	1,840	
Accumulated depreciation – computers		1,840
Narrative	Being the depreciation for the non-current assets for the year	

Task 11.8

Trial balance as at 31 December 20X8

	£	£
Capital at 1 October 20X7		36,600
Bank	32,000	
Sales		93,400
Sales ledger control a/c	30,000	
Purchases	12,000	
Purchases ledger control a/c		15,000
Advertising	10,000	
General expenses	5,500	
Prepayment – general expenses	2,500	
Rent	9,000	
Drawings	36,000	
Depreciation expense	1,840	
Irrecoverable debt expense	3,400	
Computers	2,760	
	——	——
	145,000	145,000

MOCK ASSESSMENT

1 Mock Assessment Questions

Task 1

You are working on the final accounts of a business with a year-end of 31 March 2010. Currently the business does not use a double-entry system so you are to prepare the ledger accounts for SLCA, sales tax and bank for the first time. You have the following information:

Balances	
Account	**Year-end 31/03/09**
	£
SLCA	292,887.00
PLCA	267,900.00
Sales tax owed to HMRC	32,977.00
Bank overdraft	485.00

Details for year-ended 31 March 2010

- Credit sales were £422,874.00 plus sales tax.

- Credit purchases were £303,385.00 inclusive of sales tax.

- Cash sales were £109,126.95 including sales tax.

- Receipts from receivables were £452,080.00.

- Payments to payables were £298,456.00.

- A contra was processed at the value of £9,800.00.

- The business purchased a motor car costing £31,000.00 plus sales tax and paid for it with a cheque.

- Office Expenses amounted to £590.00 exclusive of sales tax and were paid from the bank.

- The sales tax owed at 31/03/09 was paid to HMRC.

- Wages were paid that totalled £28,820.00.

- Closing balances for receivables and payables were £318,422.00 and £341,221.00 respectively.

- Assume a sales tax rate of 20%.

(a) **Using the figures given above, prepare the sales ledger control account for year-ended 31 March 2010. Show clearly discounts as the balancing figure.**

SLCA

Date 2010	Details	Amount £	Date 2010	Details	Amount £

(b) **Using the figures above, prepare the sales tax account for year-ended 31 March 2010. Show clearly the carried down figure.**

Sales tax

Date 2010	Details	Amount £	Date 2010	Details	Amount £

(c) **Using the figures above, prepare the bank account for year-ended 31 March 2010. Show clearly the carried down figure.**

Bank

Date 2010	Details	Amount £	Date 2010	Details	Amount £

Task 2

This is a task about calculating missing balances.

A sales margin of 30% applies to the business.

Sales in the period amounted to £356,455.

Purchases amounted to £213,699.50.

Closing inventory amounted to £45,382.

(a) **Draw up the trading account clearly showing the figure for opening inventory.**

Trading account	£	£

(b) **Using the information in the table below calculate the capital invested during the year. At the start of the year the balance on the capital account was £43,000.**

Assets and Liabilities at year-end 2010	£
Motor vehicles	130,000.00
Inventory	45,760.00
Receivables	97,447.00
Bank	11,978.00
Payables	65,398.00
Loan	20,000.00
Capital	?
Profit	148,677.00
Drawings	6,890.00

(c) **Tick the boxes to show what effect this transaction will have on the balances:**

A decrease in the allowance for doubtful debts.

Account name	Debit ✓	Credit ✓	No change ✓
Allowance for doubtful debts			
SLCA			
Allowance for doubtful debts adjustment			
Revenue			

(d) **Choose one statement of financial position classification for each account.**

Account name	Non-current assets ✓	Non-current liability ✓	Current asset ✓	Current liability ✓
Sales tax refund				
Land				
SLCA				
Loan: repayment due in 11 months				

Task 3

Section 2 of this exam is based on a partnership made up of three partners – Brett, Mat and Bernard. You are completing the accounts related to years ending 31 March 2010.

General Information:

- At the beginning of the financial year ending 31 March 2009, the profit sharing ratio was as follows:

  Brett – 40%

  Mat – 20%

  Bernard – 40%

- Bernard left the partnership on 31 December 2009. Goodwill was valued at £250,000 on this date.

- For the rest of the financial year ending 31 March 2010, the profit sharing ratio for Brett and Mat was 3:1.

Trial balance as at 31 March 2010		
	Dr	*Cr*
	£	£
Accruals		452
Administration expenses	35,879	
Allowance for doubtful debts		1,300
Allowance for doubtful debts adjustment		344
Bank		198
Capital – Brett		80,000
Capital – Mat		40,000
Cash	5,800	
Closing inventory	2,350	2,350
Current – Brett	1,340	
Current – Mat		4,120
Depreciation charge	9,990	
Discounts received		422
Disposal	4,300	
Equipment cost	227,000	
Equipment accumulated depreciation		46,700
Heat, light and gas	6,670	
Loan		34,000
Opening inventory	3,700	
PLCA		95,630
Prepayment	2,000	
Purchases	296,789	
Purchase returns		2,346
Rent	8,000	
Revenue		475,632
Sales returns	1,646	
SLCA	103,450	
Sales tax		14,620
Wages	89,200	
	798,114	798,114

Prepare the statement of profit or loss for the partnership for the year-ended 31 March 2010 based on the trial balance above. All year-end adjustments have been made.

	£	£
Revenue		
Cost of sales		
Gross profit		
Expenses		
Profit for the year		

Task 4

(a) **You need to prepare the appropriation account for the partnership for the year-ended 31 March 2010.**

Further information:

Salaries:

Brett – £8,000 per annum

Bernard – £6,000 per annum

Interest on capital awarded at 4% per annum. Brett and Mat's capital did not change during the year. Bernard had a balance of £50,000 on his capital account from the beginning of the year until he left the partnership.

	01/04/09-31/12/09	01/01/10-31/03/10	Total
Profit for the year			
Salaries:			
Interest on capital			
Residual profit			
Profit share:			

(b)   **Complete Bernard's capital account to deal with his retirement on 31 December 2009. It has been agreed that £10,000 will be paid straight to him and the remainder set up as a loan to the partnership.**

Further information:

The **final balance** on Bernard's current account was £3,660 (credit)

CAPITAL – BERNARD

Date 2010	Details	Amount £	Date 2010	Details	Amount £

(c)   **Complete the goodwill account to deal with Bernard leaving the partnership on 1 November 2010.**

GOODWILL

Date 2010	Details	Amount £	Date 2010	Details	Amount £

Task 5

Financial year-ending 31 March 2011

- Richard joined the partnership on 1 November 2010. Goodwill was valued at £200,000 on this date and Richard invested £30,000 into the partnership

- For the rest of the financial year, the profit sharing ratio was as follows:

    Brett – 13/20

    Mat – 5/20

    Richard – 2/20

Trial balance as at 31 March 2011		
	Dr	Cr
	£	£
Accruals		366
Administration expenses	23,245	
Allowance for doubtful debts		1,300
Bank		755
Capital – Brett		120,000
Capital – Mat		60,000
Capital – Richard		30,000
Cash	3,873	
Closing inventory	2,170	2,170
Current – Brett	1,480	
Current – Mat		18,070
Current – Richard		1,200
Depreciation charge	7,100	
Equipment cost	290,500	
Equipment accumulated depreciation		56,690
Heat, light and gas	7,200	
Loan		28,000
Opening inventory	2,350	
PLCA		52,342
Purchases	314,577	
Rent	9,000	
Revenue		544,512
SLCA	157,200	
Sales tax		5,390
Wages	102,100	
	920,795	920,795

All adjustments have been made in the trial balance above for the year-ended 31 March 2011 apart from the share of profits.

Profit for the year has been calculated as follows:

Brett – £57,452.90

Mat – £20,277.50

Richard – £3,379.60

(a) **What are the updated current account figures for the three Partners?**

	£
Brett	
Mat	
Richard	

Workings

(b) **Prepare a statement of financial position for the partnership as at 31 March 2010 including the above amendment to the current accounts.**

	£	£	£
Non-current assets			
Current assets			
Current liabilities			
Net current assets			
Non-current liabilities			
Net assets			

1 Mock Assessment Answers

Task 1

(a)

SLCA

Date 2010	Details	Amount £	Date 2010	Details	Amount £
1/04/09	Bal b/d	292,887.00	31/03/10	Bank	452,080.00
31/03/10	Sales	507,448.80		Contra	9,800.00
				Discounts	20,033.80
				Bal c/d	318,422.00
		800,335.80			800,335.80

Credit sales = £422,874 plus 20% sales tax = £507,488.80

(b)

Sales tax

Date 2010	Details	Amount £	Date 2010	Details	Amount £
31/03/10	Purchases	50,564.16	1/04/09	Bal b/d	32,977.00
31/03/10	Office exp.	118.00	31/03/10	Credit sales	84,574.80
31/03/10	Bank	32,977.00	31/03/10	Cash sales	18,187.82
	Bal c/d	52,080.46			
		135,739.62			135,739.62

Sales tax on purchases = £303,385 × 20/120 = £50,564.16

Sales tax on office expenses = £590 × 20% = £118.00

Sales tax on credit sales = £422,874 × 20% = £84,574.8

Sales tax on cash sales = £109,126.95 × 20/120 = £18,187.82

(c)

Bank

Date 2010	Details	Amount £	Date 2010	Details	Amount £
31/03/10	Sales	109,126.95	01/04/09	Bal b/d	485.00
31/03/10	SLCA	452,080.00	31/03/10	PLCA	298,456.00
			31/03/10	Motor vehicles	37,200.00
			31/03/10	Office exps	708.00
			31/03/10	Sales tax	32,977.00
			31/03/10	Wages	28,820.00
				Bal c/d	162,560.95
		561,206.95			561,206.95

Motor vehicle cost = £31,000 plus 20% sales tax = £37,200.

Office expenses = £590 plus 20% sales tax = £708

Task 2

(a)

Trading account	£	£	%
Revenue		356,455.00	100
Opening inventory (bal. fig.)	81,201.00		
Purchases	213,699.50		
Closing inventory	(45,382.00)		
Cost of sales (356,455.00 × 70/100)		249,518.50	70
Gross profit (356,455.00 × 30/100)		106,936.50	30

(b)

	£
Opening capital	43,000
Capital introduced	15,000
Add profit	148,677
Less drawings	6,890
	———
Net assets	199,787
	———

(c)

Account name	Debit ✓	Credit ✓	No change ✓
Allowance for doubtful debts	✓		
SLCA			✓
Allowance for doubtful debts adjustment		✓	
Revenue			✓

(d)

Account name	Non-current assets ✓	Non-current liability ✓	Current asset ✓	Current liability ✓
Sales tax refund			✓	
Land	✓			
SLCA			✓	
Loan: repayment due in 11 months				✓

Task 3

	£	£
Revenue (W1)		473,986
Cost of sales		
Opening inventory	3,700	
Purchases (W2)	294,443	
Closing inventory	(2,350)	295,793
Gross profit		178,193
Sundry income		
Discounts received		422
Allowance for doubtful debt adjustment		344
Expenses		
Administration expenses	35,879	
Depreciation charge	9,990	
Disposal	4,300	
Heat, light and gas	6,670	
Rent	8,000	
Wages	89,200	154,039
Profit for the year		24,920

Workings:

(W1)	£
Revenue per TB	475,632
Less: sales returns per TB	(1,646)
	473,986

(W2)	£
Purchases per TB	296,789
Less: purchase returns per TB	(2,346)
	294,443

Task 4

(a) Prepare the appropriation account

	01/04/09-31/12/09	01/01/010-31/03/10	Total
Profit for the year	18,690.00	6,230.00	24,920.00
Salaries:			
Brett	6,000.00	2,000.00	8,000.00
Bernard	4,500.00	0.00	4,500.00
Mat	0.00	0.00	0.00
Interest on capital			
Brett	2,400.00	800.00	3,200.00
Bernard	1,500.00	0.00	1,500.00
Mat	1,200.00	400.00	1,600.00
Residual Profit	3,090.00	3,030.00	6,120.00
Profit share:			
Brett	1,236.00	2,272.50	3,508.50
Bernard	1,236.00	0	1,236.00
Mat	618.00	757.50	1,375.50

(b) **Prepare Bernard's capital account**

CAPITAL – BERNARD

Date 2010	Details	Amount £	Date 2010	Details	Amount £
31/03/10	Bank	10,000	1/04/09	Bal b/d	50,000
31/03/10	Loan	143,660	31/03/10	Current a/c	3,660
			31/03/10	Goodwill	100,000
		153,660			153,660

(c) **Complete the goodwill account**

GOODWILL

Date 2010	Details	Amount £	Date 2010	Details	Amount £
31/03/10	Capital – Brett	100,000	31/03/10	Capital – Brett	187,500
	Capital – Mat	50,000		Capital – Mat	62,500
	Capital – Bernard	100,000			
		250,000			250,000

Task 5

(a)

	£
Brett (−1,480 + 57,452.90)	55,972.90
Mat (18,070 + 20,277.50)	38,347.50
Richard (1,200 + 3,379.60)	4,579.60

(b)

	£	£	£
Non-current assets			
Equipment	290,500	56,690	**233,810**
Current assets			
Inventory		2,170	
Receivables (W1)		155,900	
Cash		3,873	
		161,943	
Current liabilities			
Payables		52,342	
Sales tax		5,390	
Accruals		366	
Bank		755	
		58,853	
Net current assets			**103,090**
Non-current liabilities			
Loan			28,000
Net assets			**308,900**
Capital – Brett			120,000
Capital – Mat			60,000
Capital – Richard			30,000
Current – Brett			55,973
Current – Mat			38,347
Current – Richard			4,580
			308,900

Workings:

(W1)	£
SLCA per TB	157,200
Less: allowance for doubtful debt	(1,300)
Receivables	155,900

INDEX